ROGER FERGUSON

FINALLY!

PERFORMANCE ASSESSMENT THAT WORKS!

BIG **5** PERFORMANCE MANAGEMENT™

ISBN-10: 1491098880
ISBN-13: 9781491098882

Library of Congress Control Number: 2013914150
CreateSpace Independent Publishing Platform
North Charleston, SC

Artwork by Brooke Bowman at www.babdesignstudio.com.
Photography by Chantal Erickson at www.chantalerickson.com.

THANK YOU

This is to acknowledge and thank the five best managers I have ever had the pleasure of working for.

Barbara Rubenstein
Thank you for giving me a solid foundation in how to manage myself and others. I have always tried to follow your lead in treating people with kindness and respect.

Doug Thorpe
Thank you, Doug, for being an outstanding boss and a great friend and accountability partner. Your counsel and friendship continue to mean a great deal to me.

Cathy Nunnally
There are so many adjectives I would use to describe you: smart, driven, giving, caring, capable, connected, versatile—and the list goes on and on. You have truly been a source of ongoing inspiration in both my personal and professional life.

Scott McLean
You are easily the most outstanding executive I have ever had the privilege to work with! Your openness and active solicitation of coaching to improve your game sets you apart. Call it emotional intelligence, great leadership, or just good common sense. You are a class act.

Jeff Uribe

Thank you, Jeff, for the opportunity to participate in one of the greatest adventures of my life in Afghanistan. I appreciate your coaching and admire your skill in delivering direct messages and producing superior results. Thanks for teaching me a new way to get things done.

And a special thanks to Rick Gillis

Thank you, Rick, for your entrepreneurial spirit, your great advice, and your positive encouragement to share *Big Five*!

TABLE OF CONTENTS

INTRODUCTION

Finally! speaks to three audiences.

First, it speaks to EMPLOYEES who work in the corporate world and may not always know how to calculate or communicate the value they bring to their organizations, how to prioritize their work, or how they will get through one more year of elaborate but less than meaningful performance assessments.

Second, it speaks to MANAGERS who struggle to effectively align the efforts of their team members, are not always comfortable with confrontation when coaching or providing corrective action feedback to team members, and dread the thought of having to prepare one more round of annual performance assessments.

And third, it speaks to ORGANIZATIONS and their Human Resources Departments who continue those same tired performance assessment processes, probably because they have not found a better alternative!

Finally! introduces *Big Five Performance Management*, a novel approach to performance assessment that is faster, more effective, and creates better accountability and overall results than traditional annual performance assessment. Simply put, *Big Five Performance Management* asks employees to answer two straightforward questions: what were your five most significant accomplishments from last month, and what are your five highest priorities for next month? As simple as that might seem on the surface, *Big Five* effectively changes the complex world of performance assessment for all three audiences!

1

WHY TRADITIONAL PERFORMANCE ASSESSMENT FAILS

I am cynical but not without reason. I had taken the time from a very busy schedule to attend a Human Resources round table. If you are unfamiliar with the term, an HR round table is a meeting sponsored by a Human Resources consultant or vendor, usually at a fairly nice venue, with hopes of attracting enough decision makers from different companies to come together at one time and in one place to be able to buy their services. The affair is pitched as a sharing opportunity where there can be a free exchange of ideas and best practices. While some ideas are shared in these meetings, the primary goal is for the vendor to build client relationships, helping them separate sales prospects from sales suspects. The secondary goal is for out-of-work HR types to network and find jobs. Like I said, I am cynical. Still, these meetings produce an occasional pearl, so I put my cynicism aside and sent my RSVP.

The topic was intriguing. A well-known international oil-field services and manufacturing company was to reveal its revolutionary process for assessing employee performance and tying that performance to the employee's compensation. They actually used the word "revolutionary" when advertising the program. I was particularly interested in performance assessment as this topic had garnered a lot of attention and created a lot of angst at the two Fortune 500 companies where I had worked in Human Resources, one in the financial-services sector, the other in engineering. If smart people like bankers and engineers struggled with this issue, I wondered if manufacturers had managed to build a better mousetrap.

The vice-president of Human Resources for the company opened the session by again using the word "revolutionary." He then marched us through fifty pages of PowerPoint details.

To summarize, the performance assessment program he presented

- required each employee to write specific goals tying their individual performance to the corporate objectives for the year;

- required quantifiable metrics to determine the level of success each employee achieved in accomplishing those goals;

- allowed an optional midyear review for the employee and their supervisor to check on progress and agree on midyear course corrections;

- provided a numeric scale using a five-point system that would, at the end of the year, grade the employee by assigning him or her a cumulative, overall score—4.36, for example;

- and finally, converted the employee's overall score to an equivalent percentage in pay increase. So an overall score of 4.36 might have equaled a 5.5 percent pay increase, following an annually adjusted template created by the company.

The process was logical, ordered, and rational. So why was I cynical? I was cynical because this "revolutionary" program was the exact same performance assessment program we had created twenty-five years ago, when I was just beginning my Human Resources career!

So what is wrong with this "new" process? Nothing. It will work well as long as every level of management, from the CEO to the shop foreman, believes in it, documents it skillfully, and works proactively to make it successful. It will work well if all the employees see their annual assessment as a valuable, meaningful, and worthwhile exercise. It will work well if the feedback provided is balanced, realistic, and free of any content that might cause labor attorneys to twitch. But the more glaring and common problems with this program can be summarized in what I call the "Dirty Dozen" problems inherent in traditional annual performance assessment.

The "Dirty Dozen" Traditional Performance Assessment Challenges

1. Tying individual goals to corporate goals is difficult if not impossible.

Most corporate goals are not defined specifically enough to translate well to individual performance. This makes it difficult for the average employee to relate. A goal like "Expand our presence in the North Sea" might be a good and viable goal for a large oil company, but average plant superintendents working in US refineries cannot relate to how they might contribute to that goal, much less administrative assistants working in the corporate office.

2. Goals are seldom reliable for an entire year.

Changes in the market, competition, law, management, and technology all make annual goal setting a tedious process. The business environment changes much more quickly than our ability to manage and change our annual performance assessment goals.

3. Metrics do not always tell the entire story.

Widget producers on an assembly line can be measured by item count and scrap rate, salespeople by total sales or even by effort statistics (the number of sales calls made per month). Having a quota that describes the specific result each employee is required to produce certainly makes the evaluation of that employee an easier task for managers. There are very few jobs, however, where those behaviors and outcomes can be precisely measured. Think about the last employee you know who was unsuccessful in his or her job. Was it because the employee could not meet their quota? It is possible, of course, but most of the negative performance situations I have dealt with in my HR career involved people who did not possess good emotional intelligence, were not good team members, had personal issues that distracted them from work, were insubordinate, committed policy violations, had lost trust in their management, and so on. Metrics don't always tell the full story, and most jobs just don't lend themselves to specific, precise measurement.

4. Even the best metrics can be manipulated by the employee.

"Yes, Bob, I will place your order for the fifty cases of paper, but can it wait until Monday? I have already met my sales quota for May, and Monday is June 1, the start of my new assessment period."

5. Metrics are also subject to manipulation by management.

A numeric scale for rating employee performance that translates to a specific percentage of pay increase would appear to bring accuracy and fairness to the process. There are two challenges, however. Rater bias is the most obvious. Some managers are simply more critical, or truthful, than others. How do we account for that bias to ensure consistency across the organization in a formula-driven compensation environment? It is difficult if not impossible. Additionally, most of the managers I know who have participated in this type of process will complete it according to the established procedures, then step back and examine the results for impact and common sense: "I thought I rated everyone fairly, but with these ratings, Steve will be making more money than Alice. That is just not fair. I need to adjust the score for one or both of them to make certain that the compensation is fair."

Some organizations even have a formal process established for an official management review of the numbers managers are submitting, just to make sure that they make sense. It is ironic that even those organizations that have firmly established metrics as the basis of their performance assessments often have to conduct review meetings to overcome the inherent weakness in this type of process!

6. This is not an employee driven process.
The entire process can occur without any real involvement on the part of the employee. I have known of cases where assessments were completed and placed in the employee's file but were never shared with the employee.

7. Annual feedback is a very dated concept.
With all of the electronic communication technology available to us today (Twitter, Facebook, LinkedIn, and other

social media), most employees are accustomed to almost instant feedback. Anything more than a couple of weeks old is "yesterday's news" and no longer viewed as relevant by most employees.

8. Managers spend too much time on the process.
Managers spend huge amounts of time on this process but, generally speaking, do not believe that it adds value. It is the least pleasant aspect of their job and many times results in more conflict than improvement. And let's face facts. Most managers do not do a good job of delivering constructive criticism to employees. The combination of requiring significant preparation time and managerial difficulty in delivering bad news, means that many traditional annual performance assessments are tempered or watered down to the point where they do not truly represent the employee's value, or lack thereof, to the organization. For most managers, traditional annual performance assessment is among the lowest of all their priorities.

9. Employees are skeptical of the process.
Everyone says that they want feedback on their job performance, but do you know anyone who looks forward to this process? I think that the underlying psychological driver is that every employee wants POSITIVE feedback. Few look forward to constructive criticism. The standing joke among HR professionals who design systems like these is that the employees who welcome constructive feedback or criticism on their performance are almost always the

employees who need the least coaching! Employees who actively seek coaching, after all, are probably not waiting until year-end to find out how they are performing. Instead, they are checking in with their managers every month or two, possibly even making a nuisance of themselves, trying to get a read on how they are performing. Most employees don't actively seek out coaching and consider the annual performance assessment as a waste of time.

10. At some point in the management hierarchy, the process breaks down.

CEOs in most organizations don't prepare formal evaluations for their direct reports, and they do not receive them either. At some level in every organization, the process ceases to function properly, creating discontent in middle management: "Why should I have to do this for my team if my boss does not do it for me?"

11. The process can create corporate liability.

Performance documentation is supposed to ensure consistent and fair treatment that will help protect a company from being charged with discriminatory labor practices. When traditional annual performance assessment is done poorly, it can actually be worse for the employer than if the employer had no documentation at all! When managers are hesitant to document the facts or are uncomfortable confronting the employee, their diluted performance assessments can actually create corporate liability.

12. It is difficult to tie performance to compensation.
Annual merit compensation increase decisions for most employees in a large corporation are not driven by employee performance but by the merit increase budget. If the pool for this year is 4 percent, it is very difficult for the average employee, who is not on an incentive or bonus plan, to make significantly more. This failure to link performance to pay causes the average employee and his or her manager to doubt the value of the entire process.

So what are we to do? Attorneys insist on documentation and employees continue to say that they want feedback on their performance. How have the best employers in the world met this challenge?

There appears to be two schools of thought. The first, and most popular, is best represented by the manufacturing-company story above. Most companies attempt to create some sort of alignment between personal goals and corporate objectives using quantifiable metrics to shore up the process, making it as legally unassailable as possible. These efforts may not result in a perfect process, but they do create order, logic, and apparent fairness. Attorneys tend to like them, except when employees who have been terminated for poor performance show up in court with years of those tempered, watered down, favorable performance assessments in hand.

Managers are becoming more sophisticated in preparing and delivering the product. Their roles in the process have become so repetitive and routine that they can now depend on technology for assistance. There are several books and software packages available for purchase that allow managers to simply copy and paste predetermined comments, phrases, and paragraphs that are most often used in performance appraisals. Spelling, content, and political correctness are all guaranteed.

Employees know the drill and, for the most part, practice patience and conformity in completing the process. But the bottom line with this type of program is that just about everyone involved sees the process as a compliance exercise only. The reason they participate is because Human Resources requires it. Don't believe it? Check the metrics in your own HR department. HR will ALWAYS track which employees and managers have completed the process and which have not. The HR department will RARELY track the quality of the effort. It doesn't really matter what is said in the assessment, as long as it is completed! The only exception is when the manager includes something in the appraisal that creates attention or hints of discrimination—"Janet has a great energy level for someone her age!"—or is totally outrageous—"Bob doesn't sweat much for a big guy!" Yes, these kinds of comments are not unusual.

The other school of thought, which is smaller but growing, is to eliminate performance assessments altogether. But companies that have eliminated traditional performance assessment face a different set of challenges. How does the company ensure that managers have communicated corporate expectations to employees? How does the company know if their managers are providing adequate coaching and guidance? And what is the basis for annual merit increases or other compensation decisions? How does the company prevent favoritism and potential discrimination?

There is another option, a hybrid of the two schools that not only allows the manager and employee to have meaningful, ongoing dialogue about performance but also satisfies the Legal Department's requirements for documentation. It also takes less time than traditional performance appraisal, and all who have used it would argue that is it is certainly more effective. It has the added benefits of helping managers manage the performance of their team, independent of formal annual performance assessment, and helps all of us better manage our priorities and our time. While I am not sure it is "revolutionary," it comes close. I call it *Big Five Performance Management.*

• • •

FREQUENTLY ASKED QUESTION

WHAT IS BIG FIVE PERFORMANCE MANAGEMENT?

Big Five is a simple process that asks each employee to identify his or her five most significant accomplishments from the last reporting period and five highest priorities for the next reporting period. Big Five is useful as a performance assessment tool, a performance management tool, and as a time management tool.

2

WHY BIG FIVE PERFORMANCE MANAGEMENT WORKS

Big Five Performance Management is born from the sales culture. Effective sales teams have created practices that make them nimble and focused, creating a sense of urgency and holding team members accountable for their contributions to the teams' missions and goals. They do this by following a number of disciplined processes and procedures, but the most common is the weekly sales meeting.

Most successful sales teams meet early on Monday morning, allowing team members the time to grab their coffee and organize their weekly calendars before they begin. In this meeting, sales associates are required to provide very specific and concise action plans for the week. These plans will vary from team to team but most require reporting on

- outstanding items from the prior week;

- this week's planned action items with existing customers to maintain, increase, or "rescue" business;

- and any specific actions to take place that week that will identify, develop, or close business with prospective new clients.

The meetings are beneficial for sharing information within the team in order to better leverage the network of each team member: "I heard that ACME is going to purchase AJAX and their merger will provide us with some great opportunities. Do we know anyone at ACME?"

The meetings also allow managers the opportunity to provide team members with assistance, guidance, and coaching for any difficult clients or situations they may be facing. When well facilitated, these meetings enable collaborative success for the team and development opportunities for its members. These meetings tend to last for ten to twenty minutes only, and the achievements and expectations for that week's activities are recorded on a whiteboard or electronically for everyone in the office to see and share. Some teams ensure that their meetings are focused and quick by conducting them standing up—no chairs allowed. In other words, this meeting is not about getting comfortable; it is about pushing the proverbial football over the goal line.

The key to the success of these meetings is that everyone is required to be very specific about the actions they will take that week to move the business forward. Statements like "I need to call Mr. Jones this week" or "I might try to take Sheila Granger to lunch to discuss the deal" are not acceptable. In successful sales teams, members are evaluated on the results they produce, not their intentions. "I will talk to Mr. Jones today before noon" is the expected vernacular, and statements like "Sheila Granger and I are having lunch at the Petroleum Club on Thursday" show commitment to the action. These commitments take on special significance when they are recorded and shared with the team, creating public accountability.

Public accountability can be a very powerful tool for leadership at all levels. I am reminded of a story told about a legendary retired CEO of one of the largest and most successful regional banking enterprises in the country in the 1980s. He commanded a squadron of bombers in World War II and was disappointed that some of his pilots were dropping their payloads earlier than anticipated, well short of their targets, because of thickening enemy antiaircraft fire concentrated around each target. How did he resolve this problem? At the mission debriefing that all the flight crews were required to attend, he posted large aerial photographs showing each bomber's intended target and where it actually dropped its payload. The gap between the two closed immediately thereafter; no one wanted to endure the public ridicule of having "chickened out." That is one of the key duties of a sales manager: holding sales team members accountable for their actions and results. How?

The sales team reconvenes at the end of the week, usually on Friday afternoon, to report on the success of its efforts that week. Accountability is public and in real time. If you did not perform the actions you promised on Monday, then Friday is a day of reckoning, where you have to account for your lack of performance. Everyone will know whether you hit the target or not. Some sales teams actually complete this ritual daily and meet for a short time at the beginning and/or end of each day.

The meetings do more than just provide "the stick" of public accountability. They also provide "the carrot" of giving employees the opportunity to take credit for their accomplishments. All of us have probably worked for a boss who we believed had no idea how hard we were working, how much we were contributing, or how smart and creative we were. Or worse, we've had some managers that actually listened to our ideas and then took personal credit for them later! Remember being in the first grade? You drew that almost discernible picture of a horse (or dog, or cat, or cow) and your parents proudly displayed it on the refrigerator door so that Uncle Bill, Aunt Ruth, and all of the neighbors could comment on your artistic prowess. Deep down, all of us feel the need for approval and validation. It is one of the keys to improving employee engagement and the employee value proposition. The sales meeting provides a mechanism to enable that validation. Many employees actually look forward to the meetings so they can communicate their contributions and value to their team and their manager. At the end of the day, we all want our picture on that refrigerator door!

So what can the performance assessment world learn from sales? Are we really suggesting daily or even weekly performance assessment meetings? Of course not, but the same principles that drive sales team success apply to performance assessment. *Big Five* promotes performance assessment that, like sales, is quick and meaningful, focuses the employee's efforts on the highest priorities, and creates accountability for better overall management of the company. Finally, performance assessment that works!

• • •

3

BIG FIVE PERFORMANCE MANAGEMENT STRUCTURE

Traditional performance assessment systems tend to rate employees on some combination of the following.

Personal Production, Contribution, or Accomplishments
This category attempts to answer the question, "What or how much was produced?" This will include the completion of individual, team, and corporate goals.

Competencies or Values
This category considers the competencies of the employee, attempting to measure the behavioral skills the employee demonstrated while completing his or her work. These usually include behaviors like teamwork, adaptability, attention to safety, etc. So this category attempts to document not WHAT the employee produced, but HOW

WELL the employee demonstrated the corporate values—sometimes written and published, sometimes implied in the organization's culture—answering the question, "Did the employee work and play well with others?" Or the opposite, did this employee leave a trail of occupational death and destruction along the way?

Training and Development
This category attempts to measure any training or development activities completed by the employee: "What did the employee do to improve his or her capacity to produce more (or higher quality) work in the future?"

These are all important areas of concern, and it would be difficult to build a logical argument for excluding any of them. Still, the problems and challenges with traditional annual performance appraisal remain. Goals change too frequently to track and modify them accurately; an employee can demonstrate competency in many or all of the company-identified categories and still not be effective, and training alone rarely fixes a "broken" employee. The complexities of the traditional performance assessment process can sometimes overwhelm the purpose, making the juice not worth the squeeze!

Big Five Performance Management™ is different in that it asks employees to own the process of documenting their plans and contributions by answering two straightforward questions:

"What are the five most significant contributions the employee has made in the last reporting period?"

"What are the five highest priorities for the employee for the next reporting period?"

Can the process really be this simple? Yes, it can. Here's how.

Reporting Periods

OK, the idea of daily or even weekly performance assessment might be extreme and better left to sales teams! For use as a performance assessment tool, monthly reporting is recommended. A monthly schedule works well for performance assessment for the following reasons:

- A monthly schedule provides relevant data and feedback. No manager's feedback, coaching, or documentation will be older than thirty days.

- Monthly reporting is nothing new, as many employees are probably already producing some sort of monthly summary of their activities. One key to the success of *Big Five Performance Management* is that employees do not see this process as onerous or adding to their existing workload. The process will be much more effective when presented to employees as an improvement to the existing reporting process, saving them time and eliminating the pains of the traditional annual assessment process.

- Monthly reporting provides the manager with ample time to offer coaching, assistance, and course corrections before annual performance assessments and compensation decisions are required. This assumes that you will want to continue tying annual compensation decisions to performance, a process we will discuss later.

- Monthly reporting provides the managers with more opportunities to praise and reinforce positive employee behaviors, improving employee engagement.

- Most managers can easily handle the monthly volume, assuming they have no more than eight to ten direct reports. Reporting can be required more frequently, but remember the dangers of traditional performance assessment. If the process creates administrivia that is not perceived as valuable for both the employee and the manager, then it will degenerate into a compliance exercise only.

FREQUENTLY ASKED QUESTION

CAN BIG FIVE REPORTING REALLY BE DONE WEEKLY? WON'T EMPLOYEES REBEL IF WE ASK THEM TO REPORT WEEKLY?

Monthly reporting is recommended when Big Five is used as a performance assessment tool, but yes, weekly reporting can be effective when Big Five is used for performance management. What's the difference? The most common use of Big Five in a performance management situation occurs when new managers are sent into cleanup or turnaround situations. In those types of potentially negative situations, Big Five can be conducted on a weekly basis to help management get a better, quicker handle on who is doing what in the troubled organization.

Medium

One of the best things about *Big Five Performance Management* is that it requires no special forms or software. Employees produce their monthly reports in the form of an e-mail or Word document that they forward to their immediate supervisor making this process particularly attractive for smaller and mid-sized businesses that do not operate large HR software systems. Each monthly report should be no longer than one page in length. Bullet points and brief descriptions are recommended over lengthy narratives. The structure of the report can be less formal than traditional annual performance assessment as the content is more important than the format.

Number of Accomplishments and Priorities

How many accomplishments and priorities should the employee list each month? The answer is five: the five most significant accomplishments from last month and the five highest priorities for the upcoming month. Most employees will certainly produce more than five accomplishments per month, of course, but how many can be considered significant? The Pareto principle would suggest that only the top 20 percent of an employee's monthly accomplishments would be considered significant. The remaining 80 percent are probably those activities most associated with maintaining his or her position and meeting basic job requirements. While it is important that these activities take place, there is no value in reporting them each month. In other words, "Completed my monthly *Big Five Performance Management* report," should not appear on the list of monthly accomplishments.

FREQUENTLY ASKED QUESTION

IS THERE ANYTHING MAGIC ABOUT THE NUMBER FIVE? CAN EMPLOYEES REPORT MORE OR LESS THAN FIVE?

Experience shows that five is a good average, but there is nothing absolute about that number. An employee can report as few as three accomplishments or priorities and possibly up to seven. Managers should use common sense in coaching their employees to participate fully while limiting overly zealous employees. The bottom line is that all of the information should fit on one page. If the report is longer than one page, the process becomes tedious and can disintegrate into a compliance exercise only, not meaningful to the employee or the manager.

Due Dates

Requiring the report to be submitted by the fifth calendar day of each month is a positive way to reinforce the "five" in the *Big Five Performance Management* model. Using the fifth calendar day establishes consistency and helps to better install the process in the organizational culture.

Content Customization

While the core content *Big Five Performance Management* is a simple bullet-point list of ten items per month (five accomplishments for last month, five priorities for next month), the format can be modified to accommodate any of the components of traditional performance assessment that may be important in any specific corporate culture: team and individual goals, competencies, values, training and development, personal productivity, or even priorities related to soft skills like teamwork, innovation, and flexibility.

In his book *Love Works*, Joel Manby (www.joelmanby.com) writes that Herschend Family Entertainment, owners of Silver Dollar City Amusement Park in Branson, Missouri, rates its employees on "Kindness" in its performance assessment process. They define it as, "a measure of the employee's enthusiasm, passion, and encouragement." When norms like "Safety," "Customer Service," or even "Kindness," are important to an organization, those elements can be easily incorporated into *Big Five Performance Management*.

One manager using *Big Five* likes to vary the routine occasionally, by asking employees a thought provoking question several times a year. She does this by sending out a simple e-mail that says, "In your Big Five this month, please answer the following question. If you ran this company, what one thing would you do differently?"

See appendix A for examples of several different formats, and customize for your organization at will.

Manager Feedback

The manager's job is to reply to the employee's *Big Five Performance Management* e-mail with coaching comments that acknowledge the employee's accomplishments and encourage or redirect the employee's upcoming priorities. This response is critical to the success of the effort. The good news is that the response can be as simple and straightforward as an e-mail reply of, "Thank you for a great October! Keep up the great work, and let me know how I can help." However, the process certainly allows for continual course correction to account for rapidly changing business climates or employee performance. The manager can easily add, "Don't forget to add the Stevens account to your priorities for next month. Closing that one will mean significant revenue for us." Or "Congratulations on completing your accounting course this semester! Be sure to prepare an expense report to take advantage of the tuition reimbursement program." Or, on the negative side, "Please see me about your plans to revamp the workflow process for the solar-generator design. I am not sure I agree with your plan. Let's discuss this before you begin please." See more about the importance of the manager's response in chapter 5.

• • •

FREQUENTLY ASKED QUESTION

THIS WOULD APPEAR TO BE A RELATIVELY NEW PROCESS. HAS IT BEEN TESTED IN BUSINESS ENVIRONMENTS?

The process has been successfully implemented, either formally or informally, in business units at two Fortune 500 companies and several smaller organizations. It has been in use for approximately fifteen years.

4

DIVING INTO THE DETAILS

Now that you know the fundamentals of *Big Five Performance Management*, here are some design details you may want to incorporate.

The "Other Accomplishments" Section
Most employees will have accomplished more than the five priorities they established for the month and will need a way to track and report them. Including a section called "Other Accomplishments" in the monthly report provides a structure to accommodate that information.

The "Other Accomplishments" section is best when it appears after the report on the five most significant accomplishments for the month. Generally speaking, the narratives describing these additional accomplishments should be more concise than those describing the five most significant accomplishments.

Including an "Other Accomplishments" section not only allows the employee to better and fully demonstrate his or her value to the organization, but it also serves as an excellent historical record of what was accomplished. This information can also be useful when compiling a year-end report or responding to an audit request: "When did Susan last check our personnel files for I-9 (US government required form for employment) compliance?" That information is, most likely, included in one of Susan's *Big Five* reports.

Beware of the "overachievers" in your group who will insist on reporting a dozen or so accomplishments on multiple pages. Instruct them to throttle back to around five and include any others in the "Other Accomplishments" section. Experience shows that there should be no more than about ten "Other Accomplishments," but the number will vary according to the work environment and level of detail required in each position. Use common sense to set unofficial limits and coach your team members accordingly. Most employees can and should report ALL of their monthly accomplishments and priorities on a single typed page.

Copy and Paste
Big Five Performance Management is more efficient than traditional annual performance assessment because it takes less time to prepare. One of the reasons this is true is that the employee can begin each of his or her monthly reports by simply copying and pasting last month's priorities into this month's accomplishments—no more racking your brain in December to try and

remember everything you have accomplished this calendar year. If January's report (due on February 5 if you follow the advice for setting due dates) details the five most significant accomplishments for the month of January and the five highest priorities for the upcoming month of February, then February's report (due on March 5) should begin by describing the success or failure in completing what were identified as February priorities.

It sounds more difficult than it is. The bottom line is that if you told your manager what you were going to focus on in February, then at the end of February, your manager wants to know about the progress you made in accomplishing those priorities. This natural link of priorities and accomplishments provides a continual stream of logical connections from month to month. This will be important as we discuss how *Big Five Performance Management* can save time helping employees prepare their annual report, assuming your organization continues to require one.

So what happens if an employee is given a special project or assignment after turning in his or her five highest priorities for the month, totally changing the priorities? Once again, common sense prevails. The employee should copy and paste his or her priorities for the current month into the report and simply state that no progress was made toward those goals, explaining and documenting the situation. For example, if one of my February priorities was to "Meet with the European training vendor to see if there is potential for expanding the London program to the rest of the company's global locations," but a surprise audit made it impossible or impractical for that goal to be accomplished, then I would simply list the priority and report, "No progress made on this goal as the Peterman audit became the month's higher priority." This is not uncommon and many times simply delays the task, now making it a March priority. That is another benefit of *Big Five Performance Management*. It creates historical accountability for tasks or goals that might otherwise slip on the timeline or be forgotten totally.

Adding an SOS Section

Since the early 1900s, sailors have used "SOS" as a standard distress signal. (For trivia buffs, SOS does not actually stand for "Save Our Ship." It is simply a Morse code combination that was internationally agreed upon as a distress signal, because it was easy for telegraph operators to remember. "Save Our Ship" evolved later, because it is a good mnemonic device to help the general public remember the three letters.) Adding an SOS section in *Big Five Performance Management* provides employees with an opportunity to ask for assistance with problems or issues that they cannot address themselves. Including an SOS section is as simple as adding questions like, "What issues or obstacles are you facing? How can management assist?"

Incorporating Big Five Performance Management

Ideally, those organizations that are interested in replacing their traditional annual performance assessment process could simply bundle all twelve of the *Big Five Performance Management* monthly reports into a single electronic document, calling that document or file the employee's annual performance assessment. Assuming that the process has been completed thoroughly, the compiled document should detail the employee's specific contributions to the organization and include his or her manager's coaching comments and even some corrective action documentation for the year, if applicable. And here is the best part: **The traditional, annual performance assessment process can simply disappear, replaced by the collection of twelve monthly, rolling "mini-assessments!"** A more detailed discussion of how this might be possible appears in chapter 6.

You may, however, find yourself in a business culture or situation where your management team is not interested in totally scrapping your existing reporting or performance assessment process. Some companies have invested significant amounts of money into their performance assessment systems, and in some companies, formal goal setting and goal achievement are the well-established norms.

In organizational cultures like this, formal goal setting, metrics, dashboards, scorecards, and the like can easily be added to *Big Five Performance Management* reports. Appendix A shows some simple examples of how more traditional performance assessment components can be included in *Big Five Performance Management*.

"I'm Just a Secretary" Syndrome

You will, no doubt, have an employee who will not want to submit a monthly report because he or she is "just a secretary" (substitute any other job title you like). These employees will argue that their job description is fixed, their responsibilities are routine, and that they do not have the ability to accomplish anything report worthy for the organization. You will also hear that these employees do not have time to prepare this kind of report.

Admittedly, a typical administrative assistant is probably not going to generate income for the company by closing a big deal, designing a new product, or introducing new software. Still, every position has basic responsibilities that can be, to some degree or another, measured and reported. And process improvement is everyone's job, even for processes that may seem unimportant compared to what goes on at higher levels in the company.

There is a name to share with secretaries who think that their jobs are routine: "Colleen Barrett." Colleen was CEO Herb Kelleher's executive assistant at his law firm and joined him at Southwest Airlines, where she later became the president of the company, now one of the largest domestic airlines in the United States! The bottom line is that none of our jobs should be considered routine.

Finally, remind any employees who say that they do not have time to complete this type of monthly report that you too prepare one for your manager. If you find personal value in thinking about and ordering your monthly priorities, why would you not want to instill the same methodology in your entire organization? Employees thinking about how they can best contribute, regardless of their title or level, will almost always be a good use of time!

FREQUENTLY ASKED QUESTION

WHAT ABOUT THE SECURITY GUARD WHO MONITORS THE LOADING DOCK? HIS JOB IS VERY SIMPLE AND ROUTINE. SHOULD HE PARTICIPATE?

All employees should participate, even those in lower level, routine, or even remedial jobs. Everyone can make some form of contribution to the success of the organization, and standards of performance should be in place for all employees.

An example of a *Big Five Performance Management* report for support personnel is included in appendix A.

What if the Boss is Not on Board?

I said in the introduction that this book addresses three audiences. Admittedly, most of what has been written to this point has been directed at managers who are responsible for completing performance assessments for their individual employees. But what about employees who would like to personally adopt *Big Five Performance Management* and introduce it to their managers? In my experience, none of my prior managers have ever objected to me submitting an informal *Big Five* report to them on my own, without giving them any advance notice or asking for approval. I simply accompanied my first report with a quick e-mail note, saying, "Hey... just wanted to let you know what I was up to last month and what am I planning for next month." After all, it is important that you not only understand the value you bring to an organization but also that you are able to communicate that value to your employer. Noted job-search expert and author Rick Gillis (www.rickgillis.com) says it best in his discussions about not only finding the right job, but keeping it: "It is your professional responsibility to make decision makers aware of the value YOU bring to the organization!" *Big Five* enables that process.

In many cases where *Big Five* has been initiated by employees, the receiving managers have liked it so well that they have adopted it for their teams. It seems that everyone is interested in proving his or her value.

As a Time Management and Goal Setting Tool

I am aware of at least one situation where the receiving manager asked an employee not to "bother" the manager by submitting the monthly *Big Five* report. Do not lose heart if you find yourself in this type of situation. *Big Five Performance Management* continues to be useful to individual employees, even those who work for competency-challenged managers, as an excellent goal setting and time management tool.

I am certain you have heard the statistics before: people who have established formal goals are mathematically many times more likely to be successful than people who do not establish formal goals; and those who write them down are more likely to be successful than people who do not write them down; and those who frequently review their written goals with an accountability partner are more successful than those who don't; and so on.

I am not sure of the exact percentages, but I can tell you that I have used *Big Five* as a goal setting tool for about fifteen years and have found it to be an excellent time and priority management system. It works best when I actually write my five monthly priorities on the whiteboard in my office, tracking any progress I make on a daily basis. I also include another small section below or to the right of my *Big Five* for

"Other Accomplishments," and I list those daily as they occur. Admittedly, some of these daily "Other Accomplishments" entries never make the final report at month's end, but having tracked these priorities and accomplishments on a daily basis makes my end-of-month preparation time as short as five minutes. I rarely have to think back about anything I may have forgotten for the month.

Also, having the list in public view in my office creates an additional level of accountability, as most of my friends and colleagues know about *Big Five* and will read my board when they come in to visit, just to see what I have been up to. Their questions keep me on my toes and help me to better manage my time and priorities. And yes, there have been a number of occasions where I found myself working at eight in the evening on the fourth day of the month, just to ensure that I did not have to give myself an "incomplete" when I prepared my report on the fifth day of the month! The bottom line here is that *Big Five* works in multiple ways to ensure adequate time and attention in establishing priorities and accomplishing work.

• • •

FREQUENTLY ASKED QUESTION

HOW HAVE EMPLOYEES REACTED TO THIS PROCESS?

Employees have reacted favorably for three reasons:

Ownership

Big Five gives employees an informal and easy way to report their actions, contributions, and ideas. Employees begin to take more pride in their accomplishments and become more engaged in the success of the company.

Alignment

Big Five better aligns employees with their managers in regard to the team's priorities and objectives. Most employees appreciate the guidance, no longer having to guess or make assumptions.

Focus

Big Five helps most employees become more focused and better organized. Many employees will list their priorities and accomplishments on a whiteboard or iPad, keeping the list in sight and making daily notes on their progress. As the accomplishments mount, they begin to compete with their colleagues and themselves to produce more or better results than they did in the prior reporting period.

5

CHALLENGES TO BIG FIVE PERFORMANCE MANAGEMENT

Big Five Performance Management is an amazing process. As a time management tool, it focuses the manager and team members on their highest team priorities and enables monthly adjustments as the business landscape changes. As a performance management tool, it helps to align team goals and produces much more detailed data, as well as examples of specific accomplishments that can be shared upstream, confirming and communicating the contributions and value of the team and the team leader. And as a performance assessment tool, it replaces a very cumbersome, time-consuming system with something that is more effective than traditional annual performance assessment but requires much less time.

So is this too-good-to-be-true process too good to be true? What are the pitfalls and obstacles to its success? How might this process derail? There are four challenges to *Big Five Performance Management,* presented here in order of ascending importance.

Challenge One: Monitoring Monthly Report Completion

In traditional annual assessment systems, it is usually Human Resources that tracks the completion of the individual employee's performance assessment. Although managers should be aware of which assessments are pending, they can always count on HR to alert them if they are behind schedule. In a *Big Five Performance Management* environment, managers are more likely to have to track monthly report completion themselves, because no automated system is required. This would appear to be a significant but low value, administrative task as tracking twelve monthly reports is certainly more work than tracking one annual report.

Managers have met this challenge in several ways. First, this process can be automated and/or incorporated into existing performance assessment software. At a minimum, most allow for the attachment of a Word or .pdf document into the employee's file. The manual reports or e-mails can simply be attached to the employee's file in the system. This solution will be ideal for companies wanting to adopt *Big Five* quickly as they can start with this somewhat manual process, converting it, over time, into an automated process.

Assuming a totally manual system, the second and very simple solution is to simply delegate the task. Ask yourself, who monitors the gathering of data and statistics for your current monthly reporting process? Simply assigning the monitoring of this process to an assistant or to your second-in-command will not only relieve you of the effort but could possibly be seen as an increase in responsibility for the person assigned with the task, creating a positive, win-win situation.

Another tactic is to publish all team member reports, publicly sharing them with the team. Like the WWII bomber pilots mentioned earlier, employees are then forced into public accountability for not only completing the reports in a timely manner but also for the content of their reports. Publishing the reports will make it difficult for any one individual to bow out of the process or falsely claim responsibility for the accomplishments of another. The downside of public reporting, of course, is that employees may temper their input and exclude or dilute the information you want or need to make your business successful, because they know that others will be reading it. Still, this method can be effective. Managers who elect to publish their teams' reports will want to train their teams well and examine each report before it is published to ensure that nothing inflammatory is published; after all, conflict management can consume a lot more management time than performance assessment.

If your organization is going to insist on a cumulative, annual year-end report for each employee, then employees can simply copy and paste their "greatest hits" from each of the monthly reports, creating one annual *Big Five* report that is submitted to HR. I don't recommend this method because of its potential to create work, not streamline it. Still, doing this will shift the responsibility of tracking reports from the manager back to Human Resources.

Challenge Two: Avoiding Creep

If you do decide to adopt *Big Five Performance Management* for your organization, take every measure possible to keep the process simple. I am not sure if it is human nature or corporate preference, but someone in your company will want to add "just one more thing" to the process. These requests will repeat themselves until the process becomes so large, onerous, and top-heavy that it crumbles under its own weight, just like traditional annual performance assessment. Take every opportunity to safeguard against letting cumbersome add-ons "creep" into the process. "One page only," is the mantra.

Challenge Three: HR and Legal Department Approval

The third challenge in adopting *Big Five Performance Management* is in dealing with your own Legal and Human Resources Departments. Remember that no corporate attorney or Human Resources professional ever lost his or her job by saying, "No!" After all, risk management is a fundamental function for both departments, and aversion to risk is hardwired into the DNA of most of us HR types. Some will believe that *Big Five* is too informal a process to replace annual, traditional performance assessment and will argue that *Big Five* creates exposure and liability.

I would agree that any form of performance assessment done poorly, inconsistently, or in a discriminatory manner creates liability for the company. All other factors being equal, however, *Big Five Performance Management* creates less risk than traditional annual performance assessment. After all, what data might make the most sense to a jury in an unlawful termination case; 25 categories of checked boxes and a few narrative statements about the employee's value, or 120 examples of what the employee did or did not accomplish for the organization over the last year? A more detailed discussion of this matter is included in the next chapter.

Challenge Four: The Quality of the Manager's Response

The most significant challenge to *Big Five* is the quality of the response the manager provides to each employee's individual monthly report.

In a procurement department where *Big Five* was introduced, a midlevel manager became suspicious that his manager was not reading his monthly report, because the manager stopped responding to him. After three months without a response from his manager, he tested his hypothesis by including a fictitious accomplishment in his report, something like, "This month I managed to delegate all of my work to colleagues so that I could take it easy and cruise!" The midlevel manager embedded it in the middle of his e-mailed report so that it would not be terribly obvious. When his manager failed to respond to this comment, the midlevel manager confirmed his suspicions that his report, and probably the entire process, was meaningless.

Why does this happen? There are several possible reasons we could imagine that might help to justify the manager's non-responsiveness: lack of time or resources, lack of focus, lack of concern ("Bob is a good employee; he doesn't need me standing over him twenty-four seven"), and so on. All could factor into the manager's decision not to read or respond to the report. But the most obvious conclusion we can reach is that this manager simply did not see this process as important enough to be a priority, **one of the same challenges we see with traditional annual performance assessment!** If managers do not take the time to read, respond, and coach, then *Big Five Performance Management* will go the way of traditional annual performance assessment and will begin to be viewed as a compliance exercise only, necessary but not really useful, completed because Human Resources requires it. So how do we create and send a compelling message to our managers regarding the value of *Big Five Performance Management*, one that will stick and not fade with time or familiarity?

In my experience, I have found that managers usually focus their time and attention on four areas: making money, saving money, saving time, and resolving (or avoiding) people problems. Certainly there are other priorities that we might consider, but I would argue that things like quality, safety, customer service, employee development, and even community service are only important inasmuch as they contribute to the four larger concerns: making money, saving money, saving time, and resolving people problems. And, yes, one could easily argue that saving time is the equivalent of saving money. For purposes of this discussion, let's list it as a separate category, because not all time savings can be easily quantified in financial terms. So if we can show managers how *Big Five Performance Management* helps them to make money, save money, save time, and eliminate people problems, then they will be leading the *Big Five* parade, ensuring its success.

Making Money

Of all the arguments we might make in support of *Big Five Performance Management*, the money connection is the easiest and most logically made. After all, the very structure of the process is profit and production focused. Simply stated, employees accomplishing their highest priorities should yield the highest financial return. This would seem to be obvious, but it is the single most important reason that *Big Five* works as effectively as it does. *Big Five* focuses the organization on accomplishing its highest priorities! Assuming we have identified the correct priorities and have worked to adequately achieve them, financial success will follow. And if your organization is a not-for-profit enterprise, simply substitute the appropriate word—production, results, contributions, attendance—whatever the metric. *Big Five* is all about the bottom line!

Additionally, the financial success of the team can translate nicely to the financial success of the individual team members and their leader. When *Big Five* results and ideas are routed upstream and shared across the company, outstanding individual performers and their managers have a culturally approved and accepted method for "strutting their stuff," showing their worth, and taking credit for their accomplishments. *Big Five* helps to establish an organizational culture that makes it difficult for any manager to selfishly hide or hoard talent. *Big Five* will help managers realize that the upward mobility and promotion of their team members is not a task that they focus on once a year but one that should be incorporated into their daily or, in the case of *Big Five*, monthly management routine.

Saving Money

Managers are also more likely to embrace *Big Five Performance Management* when they understand how *Big Five* enables process improvement, thereby reducing corporate expense.

Where do the best ideas about how to improve a product, process, or customer experience come from? Although they can certainly come from the CEO or the manager of the business unit, many times they come from the operators, the workers, and the entry-level employees, who, after all, are the most familiar with the challenges of the products or process because they deal with them on a daily basis. *Big Five* enables creativity and creates a culturally accepted methodology for communicating creative ways to save money.

One of the reasons it works is that there is a curious but predictable consequence of asking employees to tell you what they have accomplished or created on a monthly basis. Team members start to compete, not just with each other but also with themselves, trying each month to better their results. This opens the door for all sorts of ideas and efforts on how to improve processes, eliminate waste, provide better customer service, and so on. All of these should contribute in some form or fashion to help managers save money and time.

But the financial benefits do not stop there. As *Big Five* reports are consolidated and shared upstream, new sources of creative and profitable ideas begin to surface. People and teams never before heard from begin to contribute ideas for improving company profitability. Best practices are shared across the company, and, like the sales culture from which *Big Five* was born, cross-selling opportunities are identified and exploited. When *Big Five* is adopted at the corporate level, it can actually improve communications and help to eliminate some of the corporate silos that sometimes separate departments within a company, causing them to work at cross-purposes. *Big Five* helps to improve communication and collaboration between departments.

Saving Time

Big Five Performance Management takes less time than traditional annual performance assessment. It particularly reduces the time required of the manager. The fact that the employees own the responsibility for the initial preparation of the monthly report saves management a considerable amount of time, of course. In addition, the manager's response to each employee's monthly report should also take less time, on average, than what is done in traditional annual performance assessment. How thoroughly should a manager respond to a typical *Big Five* monthly report? Generally speaking, managers should formally respond in a detailed fashion to the five most significant items of the employee's ten reported accomplishments and priorities. The other five can be left without a written response or given an "Atta boy!" Many times the manager's response to an employee's monthly report might be as simple as, "Congratulations on a great January! Your February priorities look good to me!" And having the option to provide minimal feedback is an important time-saver for everyone. Just how important?

A colleague at the largest online retailers in the world shared with me that she is involved in some aspect of their traditional annual performance assessment process for approximately four months of each year! A former general manager at one of the largest engineering firms in the United States reports that several years ago he tracked his total hourly involvement in the traditional annual assessment process and found that he spent four hundred hours—the equivalent of ten forty-hour workweeks—on the process! Basic Internet research shows that the average manager spends about eight hours per week or 20 percent of his or her time on performance management.

And what about the return on that time investment? Only three of every ten employees agree that their company's performance management system actually helps them improve their performance, with 85% of companies reporting that their performance management systems are only "moderately effective." Less than 40 percent of employees say that their performance management system helps to establish clear goals or generates honest feedback from their managers. Less than 45 percent of employees say that their managers provide them with fair and accurate feedback, and only 50 percent believe that their managers are effective at driving performance management in their organizations. It makes you wonder whether the board of directors or stockholders of any Fortune 500 company truly understand how many hours their highly compensated individuals are spending on a process that adds so little value.

So can a manager literally throw an occasional "Atta boy!" or "Atta girl!" response to an employee's *Big Five* monthly report and continue to make the process successful? The answer is both yes and no. Psychologists tell us that the best form of behavior modification, whether training your team members at work or your Doberman at home, is intermittent behavior modification. Intermittent means that the reinforcement or coaching varies and is not consistently critical, verbose, or detailed.

Of course, it sometimes needs to be all of those things if it is to be effective. Success lies in variation. If the manager's monthly response is always very detailed and critical, the employee will come to see the process as negative, the equivalent of a monthly trip to the woodshed and best illustrated by one of my favorite workplace quotations: "The beatings will continue until morale improves!" If the manager's response is always simple and lacks detail—for example, "Keep up the great work!"—then the process will also lose value. So the answer is yes, some months managers can provide minimal responses to employees, but some months managers need to put on their Bear Bryant fedoras, roll up their sleeves, and genuinely coach their team members using *Big Five* and by spending "face time" with those in need.

The final piece of good news is that the *Big Five* process actually creates coaching! We know that most managers will verbally acknowledge the importance of developing their employees and work hard to carve out time for this activity. We also know that some managers with very good intentions can be distracted, forgetful, conflicted by other priorities, or just have a hard time remembering that the development of their team members is important. By its very nature and structure, *Big Five Performance Management* provides a built-in opportunity for monthly coaching, assisting even the most distracted management types. Coaching is no longer an activity that managers "need to get around to" whenever they can. It is now part of their monthly management reporting process. The net effect for the manager is that they spend more time coaching and less time worrying about not being an effective coach!

FREQUENTLY ASKED QUESTION

HOW DOES BIG FIVE AFFECT EMPLOYEE COACHING?

Monthly Big Five reporting provides a structured approach to coaching that enables and reinforces the process. The bottom-line effect is that the manager spends more time coaching and less time worrying about when they are going to be able to carve out time for coaching!

And one final note on time savings. When discussing this aspect of *Big Five Performance Management*, some will ask about the increased amount of time that employees will have to spend on this process, pointing out the possibility that the total organizational time commitment has not changed but simply shifted from managers to employees. My experience tells me that even with the added employee involvement time, the *Big Five* process takes less total corporate time than traditional annual performance assessment. Even if there were no time savings, I would argue that having employees identify, order, and align their priorities is almost always a good use of time.

Preventing People Problems

In presenting the "Dirty Dozen Problems of Traditional Performance Assessment" in chapter 1, I said it pretty clearly: most managers, even good managers, are not very good at handling personal confrontation or at least are not very comfortable doing it. It's that human nature thing again. None of us wants to be perceived as the bad guy and we certainly don't enjoy having to discipline our employees. But as managers, we have all been there. At least one of our employees will apparently become incapable of making it to work on time, will treat a customer rudely, or just won't meet established sales goals, forcing our hands. And we all love the typical response from the troublemaker: "You want me to be on time? No one else comes in on time! I have been tracking everyone else in the department and noting what time they come in for two months now. Here is my list. Why do I have to be on time when no one else is on time? Is it because of my [gender, race, age, sexual preference, etc.]? Do I need to take this to Human Resources?!"

OK, I admit that this sort of response might be over the top, but it has certainly happened before, and all of us fear that we may be on the receiving end of that kind of rant. So how does *Big Five* assist with this challenge?

Unless you, as the manager, have substantially edited or totally rewritten every one of the employee's monthly priorities, the employee has had direct input on all of the priorities written in his or her monthly *Big Five* reports. The employee, for the most part, has documented the tasks he or she said were most important. Determining whether the priorities were or were not accomplished should be a fairly straightforward task, giving the manager a more solid footing on which to base his or her critique of the employee's performance. The process of holding employees accountable for results becomes easier, because the structure of *Big Five Performance Management* becomes more behaviorally focused than traditional annual performance assessment.

What does it mean to be behaviorally focused? Tune in to any network television talk show to learn more. When your eleven-year-old runs through the living room (where he has been told not to run) and accidentally breaks a one-hundred-year-old lamp, do you lose your temper, yell at the child, and call him stupid? I would hope not. Instead, you coach the child and probably discipline from the point of view that this is a "good kid" who did a "bad thing." That is the behavioral approach—attacking the behavior and not the person. And you would probably communicate it to the child in just that manner, saying things like, "I love you; you are a good kid, but you did a bad thing, and here are the consequences." There is no difference with your employees—except that you will probably want to substitute the word "love" with "respect," just to keep things professional in the workplace. After all, "I respect your efforts, but you did not accomplish the priorities" should be a relatively easy message for managers to convey to most employees.

So *Big Five* makes it easier to deal with people problems, and managers will certainly appreciate that fact. After all, people problems also tend to be large consumers of the manager's time, energy, and, in the case of formal complaints or lawsuits, their money as well!

• • •

FREQUENTLY ASKED QUESTION

WHAT ARE THE CHALLENGES OR OBSTACLES TO SUCCESSFUL IMPLEMENTATION OF BIG FIVE?

There are four:

First, as the format for the monthly report is a simple e-mail or Word document, the manager will be responsible for tracking the employee's monthly completion of the report, not HR. Automation or delegation of that task is the simplest solution.

Avoid adding additional components to Big Five as much as possible. The beauty of the process is its simplicity. Many people will want to add "just one more thing," changing the simple process into one that looks a lot like traditional, annual performance assessment.

Third, your Legal and HR Departments may prefer more formal processes, because they believe that the more formal the process, the stronger the legal case in litigation. If Legal or HR objects, remind them of the times that employees who have been terminated for poor performance have appeared in court with years of acceptable, good, or even outstanding traditional performance assessments in hand.

Finally, the manager has to make this process important. He or she does so by responding to each report in a positive manner, coaching employees on specific items that the employee has reported. If managers are not requiring, *reading, or responding to the employees' reports, the employees will quickly under-stand that this is a meaningless exercise, just like most traditional performance assessment processes.*

6

REPLACING AN ANNUAL, TRADITIONAL PERFORMANCE ASSESSMENT PROCESS

If you or your organization is considering replacing your annual, traditional performance assessment process, you will need to make three key decisions regarding implementation. They are decisions about how you will handle corrective action, overall employee evaluation, and annual compensation increases.

Corrective Action
Corrective action refers to any action on the part of the manager to document or convey dissatisfaction with an employee's performance when the continuation of that negative performance will most likely lead to the employee's termination. So corrective action is more than coaching; it is coaching with the intention of having the employee either improve

or find another job. It differs from normal daily coaching or informal training where the manager might be advising, teaching, demonstrating a skill, or simply directing traffic for the office. Corrective action is more serious, requires documentation, and should almost always involve your HR or Legal Department, because the consequences of administering it improperly can be significant.

As a result, the informal structure of *Big Five Performance Management* may not be appropriate as a replacement for your organization's formal corrective action process, usually a three-step process consisting of a verbal warning, written warning, and final warning. I recommend retaining your existing, more formal three-step process for corrective action; because legally, historical precedence will be an important consideration should you find yourself in court. In other words, if you have an established corporate history of always successfully administering your three-step corrective action process, there is value in retaining that process, as your attorneys can make the argument, "Your Honor, we have always treated these issues with the same level of care, regardless of the employee's race, color, creed, sexual preference..." If you do not have a formal three-step corrective action process in place, then *Big Five Performance Management* can be used effectively to document corrective action as long as the manager's comments are very specific about which company policies were violated, which behaviors were unacceptable, when they occurred, and what the consequences will be should the negative behavior continue.

So if you already have a formal corrective action policy in place, what role does *Big Five* play in the process? We already know that *Big Five Performance Management* provides a very efficient platform for monthly, instructional coaching. But it also helps to build a solid foundation of documentation when corrective action is required. The fact that *Big Five* performance reporting is done in smaller, monthly, bite-sized chunks and focuses on the accomplishment of specific monthly priorities means that the data found there should be much more specific than the data normally collected and presented in a traditional annual performance assessment process. After all, most traditional annual performance assessment processes do not lend themselves to documenting specific behavioral examples—those found most useful in courts of law—instead providing general information regarding the overall value of the employee to the organization.

What's the difference? A traditional annual performance assessment comment might look something like this: "Bob is a team player who works well with others and always accomplishes whatever task is assigned. It is a pleasure to have him on the team!" That's not necessarily a bad manager comment, but consider that a year's worth of *Big Five* performance reports will, on the other hand, have approximately 120 examples (ten a month for twelve months) of specific priorities that Bob did or did not accomplish, providing much more detail, including the manager's coaching and possibly some corrective action comments. That *Big Five* detail can easily be incorporated into your corrective action process, as required. Three examples of high-quality coaching comments—those that might later be used as corrective action documentation—appear below. See appendix B for more examples.

"Thanks for the extensive report on your February accomplishments, Derrick. Please remember that *Big Five* means approximately five. Please trim next month's report down to about five major accomplishments. Your entire report should fit on one page."

"Julie...nice job on the Henderson account! I appreciate you closing that deal. One caution, as we discussed, be careful about how much client information you share outside the company, as it could come back to bite you (and the company)."

"As we discussed and documented, please continue to make sure that you arrive at work by the eight o'clock start time in the morning and leave no earlier than five in the evening. Please see me if you need to alter that schedule."

FREQUENTLY ASKED QUESTION

WHAT ROLE DOES BIG FIVE PLAY IN FORMAL CORRECTIVE ACTION? CAN IT REPLACE OUR CURRENT CORRECTIVE ACTION PROCESS?

Generally speaking, the corrective action processes of most major corporations have been tested thoroughly via past legal actions. In addition, judges, attorneys, and juries in HR cases put credence in the consistency in which corrective action processes are administered. For those reasons, it is recommended that Big Five not replace the established corrective action processes. The good news is that Big Five should provide the company with enough solid, statistical, historical data to defend against any unwarranted claims.

Overall Employee Evaluation

Another decision your organization will have to make when considering the implementation of *Big Five Performance Management* in lieu of traditional annual performance assessment is how to provide an overall score or evaluation summarizing each employee's overall rank within the team or contribution to the organization. We are all familiar with these assessments. They tend to be an actual numeric score on a "one-to-some" point scale or a generic narrative rating saying that the employee has "met expectations," "exceeded expectations," or "greatly exceeded expectations" for the year. These types of overall annual ratings are common, but what purpose do they serve, and what value do they add? I could understand the value of an overall rating if an organization was intent on terminating the bottom 10 percent of its work force, but US courts have frequently determined that this type of forced or "stacked" ranking has a disparate impact on some protected classes of workers. Microsoft, for example, stopped this practice in November of 2013. I could certainly understand a ranking system or overall score if the employee's annual merit increase was tied to that score. But we have already mentioned the inherent weakness in the traditional system and will talk more about it in the next section. Is the ranking used to identify potential leaders so that they can be placed into accelerated development programs? Not in any of the Fortune 500 organizations I have worked with. So what is the value of this practice?

The answer is that ranking employees creates very little value. I would argue that the only employees who benefit from an overall rating or scoring system are those who are given the gold star, placed at the top of the charts, and given the highest scores. And these people are, generally speaking, already highly motivated! Employees scoring in the middle or lower ranges are never happy to know they are "average" and are rarely incented to improve their performance; rather, they are more likely incented to look for another job!

Big Five does not seek to assign an overall value to the employee. Instead, it focuses on what was planned and what was accomplished, simplifying the entire process. If an organization were to insist on an overall ranking or score for their employees, I would suggest a simple addition to the *Big Five Performance Management* process. At the bottom of each monthly e-mail response the manager prepares, he or she could copy and paste the check-a-line rating system below.

Manager's Monthly Performance Evaluation
___ *5- Greatly exceeded the accomplishments of monthly priorities*
___ *4- Exceeded most monthly priorities*
___ *3- Accomplished the agreed upon monthly priorities as expected*
___ *2- Accomplished some of the monthly priorities but improvement is needed*
___ *1- Unacceptable accomplishment of agreed upon priorities.*

Scores could be added, averaged, and compared just like traditional, annual performance appraisal.

Annual Compensation Increases

If your company is one that provides employees with annual merit increases in pay, you will have to decide how you will or will not **document the link** between the performance of the employee and the amount of the merit increase he or she will receive. And I use that terminology very specifically, because I believe that most of us will be unable to change how we actually link pay to performance, only how we document it. The fact of the matter is that for all positions, other than those that are strictly commission based, "management discretion" determines the amount of pay increases for each employee, regardless of the systems and processes we put in place to ensure corporate standards for fairness and equity (see "Managers Can Manipulate Metrics" in the Dirty Dozen section in chapter 1).

Furthermore, the most important factor influencing the average employee's pay increase in the corporate world is not the employee's performance. The most important driver in determining pay increases for most employees is the amount of money or percentage increase the compensation committee of the board of directors or your management team has authorized for the year. Yes, some employees have such exceptional performance or are so specialized in their function that they can command an annual pay increase of more than the allotted merit pool percentage. Most, however, cannot.

The total amount of money placed into the merit pool is calculated by taking the total number of employees in the department and assuming each will get the percentage increase approved by management. The manager's job, then, in most cases, is to make slight adjustments to that merit pool allocation number for each employee, in an effort not only to differentiate the better performers but to make certain that there is equity in pay between people in the same job title with the equivalent amount of experience. Some have to account for promotional increases from the same pool. And this can be a difficult task, because in most organizations, it is rare for an average to below average employee to receive no increase at all. Why? Once again, consider that none of us enjoys employee confrontation and today's legal climate always makes us wonder when the next discrimination charge will come. No one wants that sort of problem, of course.

This means that managers spend an inordinate amount of time trying to divide a fixed and small piece of pie, quibbling over fractions of percentages that, after taxes, sometimes have very little impact on the employee's bottom-line paycheck. Still, managers want to be fair, the company wants to stay out of legal trouble, and employees always want more, even if only a little more. So what do we do?

Big Five Performance Management will be most effective when performance and pay are treated as different subjects and addressed at separate times: performance monthly and compensation annually. An open and honest acknowledgment that performance is probably the third most important driver in determining compensation will help managers deliver a better message to employees—one that they can believe in and don't have to apologize for. Separating the performance issues from the compensation issues will help managers buy into and own the *Big Five Performance Management* process.

Don't believe that individual performance is the third most important driver? Picture yourself either giving or receiving the two compensation conversations below. While the differences are subtle, which one would you find easiest to deliver as a manager and the most believable as an employee?

Typical Performance Assessment Compensation Conversation

"Sharon, I really appreciate your time and attention today, meeting with me to complete your annual performance appraisal. I think we have covered most of the details and talked about your contributions to the team, and, for the most part, we agree on the areas you need to improve for next year. And now we get to the part I know you are most interested in…money. [This part is usually accompanied by the manager's nervous laughter!] Your merit increase percentage this year is 4 percent. I know it isn't as much as you might like, but it does raise your base pay from $56,000 to $58,240. I wish I could have given you more, but times are tough. I know the company reported record profits this year, but our department has been hard-pressed to hold the line on expenses, and this is the best

I could do. Maybe next year I can do a little more. Keep up the good work!"

Recommended Compensation Conversation, Separate from Performance

"Sharon, thanks for coming in. I wanted to talk to you today about your merit increase for next year. As you probably already know, pay increases here at ACME are influenced by three factors. First and foremost, company management looks at the market, our competitors, and similar employers to assure that our compensation levels are competitive. Second, the financial performance and condition of the company and our department are considered. As you know, the company showed record profits this year, and that certainly helped, but our department is still being pressured to hold the line on expenses. And finally, we certainly considered your individual performance and contribution to the team. Given those three factors, the company has determined the merit pool for this year to be 4 percent, and I am pleased to inform you that will be the amount of your merit increase for this year. That will take you from $56,000 to $58,240. I appreciate the contribution that you make to our team. Keep up the good work!"

My recommendation for how to handle the tie between performance and pay and the documentation of that link is, like most of the components of *Big Five Performance Management*, simple. If the compensation committee determines that the annual merit pool amount is 4 percent for this year, for example, then give every employee who is not on some sort of probation or corrective action a standard, across-the-board, announced and published 3 percent increase, reserving the additional but unannounced 1 percent for bonuses for the outstanding performers who are not already on some sort of bonus plan or incentive-pay schedule. And, of course, each company can manipulate the math so that it makes sense for them, but this fundamental model should make the entire process more palatable for everyone. It will save managers a significant amount of time—time that can be devoted to customer service, employee development, new product research, or any number of more productive and profitable activities.

But wait. Won't employees complain if they do not receive any of the 1 percent bonus money? And won't managers still spend a significant amount of time deciding how to allocate their 1 percent bonus money? Yes and yes, but not to the degree that those activities occur under a more traditional system. A significant statistical percentage of employees will understand that they are not top performers and will accept the 3 percent more readily than they have in the past. After all, the increase percentage is not so much a personal reflection of their individual value to the company but more of a business decision about what the company believes it can afford to pay. Managers will still have to spend some time deciding how to allocate the 1 percent bonus, but the number of employees who should qualify for that money, the truly outstanding performers, should be a much smaller audience and, therefore, take much less administrative time and effort. Additionally, this type of system will tend to provide more intermittent and, therefore, more effective behavior modification to high-level performers, helping to eliminate entitlement mind-sets and to drive performance. The company may also be able to slow the compounding effect of annual pay increases by making some of the pay (1% in the example above) discretionary and variable.

• • •

FREQUENTLY ASKED QUESTION

HOW ARE ANNUAL MERIT INCREASES DETERMINED WHEN USING BIG FIVE AS THE ANNUAL PERFORMANCE ASSESSMENT TOOL?

The single most important driver of compensation in an organization is not employee performance but the amount of money the company has approved or placed in the "merit increase pool." Managers in most organizations are only able or willing to make small distinctions in merit differences between high-performing, average, and low-performing employees. They also have to address equity issues from that same pool. Our advice is to give each *employee who is not on some sort of perfor-mance probation the allocated pool amount and provide SPOT (management discretion-ary) bonuses for those who are truly your best performers. We would also recommend sepa-rating performance conversations from com-pensation conversations.*

7

FINAL WORDS

In conducting research for this book, a common anecdotal theme has surfaced. All of us who have worked in the corporate world for any significant amount of time, in companies large and small, have had more negative performance assessment experiences than positive…or at least we remember them that way. Brooke's story is typical. And yes, the names have been changed but the stories are true!

In June, Brooke and her team were piloting a new training vendor and its training product in Los Angeles, and her East Coast counterparts were coming to town to participate and observe. As the event facilitator, Brooke was responsible for organizing the program and keeping it on track. The day of the event, she woke up with flu symptoms. Knowing she could not stay at home that day, she showed up and fought her way through the day, sipping DayQuil and blowing her nose.

The event was a success, or at least she thought it was, as all the feedback was very positive and no one reported that she had inadvertently infected any of her guests or coworkers. Six months later, in her first performance assessment meeting with her manager, she was told that showing up when she was ill was irresponsible and that she should have had someone available as backup. She was stunned by the revelation that she had acted "unprofessionally"; she thought that dragging herself out of her bed to ensure the success of the program was the very definition of the word "professional!" Pile on the fact that this feedback came six months after the event and, needless to say, Brooke did not consider this feedback to be positive, constructive, or motivational!

Brooke is not alone in her negative feelings about performance assessment. Angela is a private banker for a very large commercial bank in Seattle and once received a performance assessment from her new boss that was actually written for another employee! The mistaken identity issue was not discovered until a bewildered Angela mustered the courage to confront her boss two days after her performance assessment meeting. After all, the feedback she was given didn't seem to match her performance at all—oops! To her credit, the manager admitted her mistake and then presented Angela with the appropriate performance assessment, the one that was actually written for her.

Craig was a young lieutenant at Fort Benning who had completed a round of efficiency reports (ERs are the US military's equivalent of performance assessments) on each of his non-commissioned officers before leaving one military assignment for another, standard operating procedure for the US Army. Two months after Craig changed venues, a colonel called him to see if he would be willing to change a past ER, downgrading his scores for a particularly troublesome staff sergeant. It seems that the sergeant, while being technically sound in his work, had trouble working and playing well with others, particularly officers. This colonel was attempting to inflict as much pain as possible on the sergeant, because an ER score below a certain threshold number could apparently affect the sergeant's future pay and possibly his retirement benefits. Craig refused to change his rating, even after the colonel menacingly asked Craig if he intended to make a career of the army. Craig did not stay in the army, by the way.

Stephen also had a poor experience. He was a department manager in an aerospace engineering company who was unhappy with his annual performance assessment for the second year in a row. As he was preparing his strategy for responding to the "bad review," he overheard two of his colleagues discussing their dissatisfaction with their performance assessments, all prepared by the same manager. The three of them compared notes and decided to appeal their ratings to their manager's manager, the big boss, via the company's open-door policy. An investigation revealed that the manager who had prepared the three reviews was philosophically opposed to giving any performance assessment feedback or rating that was better than what his boss had given him. In his mind, no one in the department could score higher than him as his score represented the performance of the collective department. Wow!

And the Internet is full of stories and quotes about poor assessment practices, many from the military. Here are just a few of my favorite performance assessment comments. Feel free to Google the subject if you would like to see more.

"His team will follow him anywhere but only
out of morbid curiosity!"
"This lieutenant has delusions of adequacy."
"Somewhere a village is missing its idiot!"
"Not the brightest crayon in the box."
"Since my last report, this employee has not been content to
hit rock bottom. He has now started digging!"
"Maria is a great employee but I just don't give fives on
my reviews!"

So what is the point? Regardless of how well organizations attempt to formalize their annual performance assessment processes, even to military standards, the traditional process is flawed and broken. While some managers are very adept in making the process work in spite of its flaws, most do an average job of administering performance assessments, making it painful for them and for their employees, creating at least as much negative energy as positive in the process. So what are the keys to doing it well? Here is the *Big Five* advice for delivering *Big Five Performance Management* feedback to your employees:

1. No Surprises

If you, as the manager, do not think that a negative performance issue is important enough to deal with when it occurs or, assuming monthly reporting, in the month that it occurs, then it is not important enough to mention in later months or in an annual performance assessment. Have the managerial courage to deal with issues as they happen. No employee should ever be surprised by negative feedback. Surprise breeds mistrust, and mistrust will poison your relationship with your team. Build your team and your reputation for being a "straight shooter" by dealing with issues when they occur.

2. Adopt an Improvement Mind-Set

Managers are very likely to think of their team members as being high performers, average performers, or low performers. This is not uncommon, as a standard bell-shaped curve would dictate that sort of distribution for any team with a statistically significant number of players.

Why is this important? The manager's perspective on each of these groups can greatly influence how he or she provides performance feedback to members of each group. After all, it would be logical to assume that high performers need stroking to fuel their large egos and guidance to help focus their bound less energy. Low performers need motivation and training to develop their skills, or, in some cases, we might be just as content to have them voluntarily leave the organization. And average performers, well, every organization needs them, don't we? It might be better just to leave that group alone and not upset the status quo with all this performance improvement talk, right?

Managers will find that they do a much better job of performance assessment and help drive all of their team members to higher performance levels when they treat everyone with a consistent mind-set, one that is focused on improving the performance of *all* team members, regardless of their status in the high-to-low performance hierarchy. If the manager approaches each coaching event or performance assessment session with a sincere desire to help the employee improve, the message will be easier for the manager to deliver and more beneficial for the employee hearing it. This makes the process valuable, no longer a waste of time.

3. Lead by Example

It is a curious phenomenon, but one of the reasons managers are reluctant to hold employees accountable for their behavior is the manager's lack of personal integrity. That's a strong statement; I know, but consider the following:

Policy at a Fortune 500 company states that corporate credit cards are not to be used for personal purchases, only for business-related expenditures. The department that audits the use of the cards occasionally notices what appear to be personal uses of company credit cards. After all, you would expect that very few corporate charges would be made to a retail establishment specializing in designer apparel. So when those types of charges appear on a corporate credit card, managers of the employee making the charge are notified and asked to verify these transactions as corporate purchases.

The managers at this particular company, by and large, have a difficult time confronting employees on this matter, creating a large backlog of outstanding investigations. Why are these managers hesitant? You may have been able to guess that they too are accustomed to using their corporate credit cards for personal purchases! In spite of the written policy prohibitions, use of corporate cards for personal purchases appears to be the cultural norm in this company.

Now you might correctly point out that in this case, we appear to have more of a corporate-integrity issue than a personal one. Still, the example is a good one. Managers will have a difficult time coaching employees on the use of corporate credit cards when they are in violation themselves. Managers who are habitually late to work are going to have a hard time coaching their employees on the importance of punctuality. Managers who gossip and prefer office politics over production will falter when it comes to coaching employees on professionalism.

Leading your employees by demonstrating your personal willingness to adhere to whatever standards you are publicly communicating will earn you the right to be heard by your employees. Respect and credibility with your team members are important, not just for performance assessment, but for all of your interactions with your team.

4. Evaluate Accomplishments, Not Personalities

Traditional annual performance assessment fails because it many times attempts to assign an overall value, net worth, or compiled score to mark the value of a person to the organization, comparing that employee's value relative to others in the company. The danger of that kind of system is that it attempts to summarize the depth and breadth of a human being with a numeric score or a few narrative comments. And know this, please. I do not object to that effort based on any sort of righteous feeling that there is dignity in the soul of the worker, that we are all God's creatures, or that all of us are important in some way, form, or fashion. While I do believe in those things, the reason I object to an overall score is because it is just about impossible to accurately assess the value of a person in any way that truly adds value. But we keep trying.

Read any of the comments from your last performance assessment and you will find them to be generic and unspecific, even if they are positive in nature. Try it. Pick a quote from your last appraisal. If yours is typical, the quote will probably say something like, "Kay is a great employee, always reliable, a good team player, and always willing to go the extra mile. It is a pleasure to work with her!" Now, think of someone else in your organization you would consider to be a colleague or counterpart. If you substituted his or her name for yours in the comment, would the comment still make sense? For performance assessment to be truly effective, we have to stop generally evaluating people with clichés and start evaluating performance, talking exclusively about what employees have accomplished and what their accomplishments have meant to the organization.

5. Develop Emotional Intelligence

The term "emotional intelligence" or "EI," has woven itself into the fabric of today's leadership training and development, but the fundamentals of EI are as old as literature itself. To paraphrase a verse from the Old Testament book of Micah, we are all required to do what is right, love mercy, and be humble. As complex as a subject like emotional intelligence might be to some, for those in leadership roles, Micah sums it up pretty well. After all, most of the leadership failures we have seen have not been technical failures but emotional failures. Many managers have been promoted into their current positions because they have demonstrated technical expertise in the products and practices of the business. They lead the team because they seem to know the most about what needs to be done technically to make the business model successful. Where they may fail is in their personal maturity; their ability to guide, motivate, and develop others; how they handle conflict; how they react to criticism; how they respond to pressure; and, yes, sometimes, how they present performance assessment feedback.

So how do you ensure that your team members will begin to think of you as one of their best managers ever? I recommend the following actions and beg Micah's forgiveness for expounding on his three simple tenants by presenting,

"The Ten Commandments of Managerial Emotional Intelligence"

1. Do the right thing. Demonstrate the managerial courage to act as you must, not as you feel. Do not be ruled by your mood or sensitivities. React to pettiness, unjust criticism, or personal attack with an objective, open mind and a sincere desire to understand and rectify the situation, not to get even.

2. Always tell the truth, but never use the truth as a weapon to hurt others. Many times you can be at your absolute worst as a team leader, colleague, or boss when you are right about something!

3. In regard to communication, tell your team as much as you can as soon as you can, and tell as many as you can. This builds trust.

4. Seek win-win solutions. If you winning means that someone else on your team is losing, you have probably not considered all of your options.

5. Forgive mistakes quickly and leverage them to improve your processes and people. Erik Qualman (www.socialnomics.net) noted author and social media expert advises us to be "flawsome," learning how to fail quickly and turn potentially negative situations into positive outcomes. A colleague of mine sums the idea

up nicely on a sign in his office that says, "Make a new mistake today!"

6. Whenever possible, trust that people will do what they say until they prove you wrong.

7. Be patient and kind with others, as they may not be moving at your same speed. This is the essence of diversity.

8. Share credit and take the blame whenever you can., apologizing when you are wrong. You do not have to be perfect to be successful.

9. Acknowledge the contributions of your team members without feeling threatened. If you are doing a good job of hiring, you will probably always have one or two people on your team who are smarter than you are! Appreciate and celebrate the ideas and contributions of others at least as much as you do your own.

10. Practice servant leadership, putting the needs of your team members ahead of your own. Pride sometimes keeps us from making the best decisions for our teams.

The Path Forward

You have certainly noticed by now that this is not a research-based, data-driven, scholarly book. Only a few statistics from general Internet searches have been included, and no data that could be considered original research has been collected. Why not? Because you don't need a PhD, a complex set of metrics, or a linear regression analysis to know that traditional annual performance assessment is ineffective. It takes HUGE amounts of managerial time and expense while yielding very little return on investment. Employees mock it. Managers subvert it. HR departments apologize for it. In today's vernacular, traditional annual performance assessment is one hot mess!

Consider the "Big Data" numbers, please. If we assume that the manager I mentioned in Chapter Five, the one spending 400 hours per year on the traditional annual appraisal process, could save approximately 200 annual hours, 50 percent of that time, by adopting the *Big Five* process, what would the impact be on his personal productivity? This manager was at a base pay level of $250,000. If we factor in 30% in benefits and a $35,000 bonus, the total annual overhead cost for this manager is approximately $360,000. That is a per hour cost of $173.07. Two hundred hours would mean an annual savings of over $34,000 for one manager in one company! And let's assume that the manager does not simply waste those 200 hours shopping on-line but dedicates them to tasks like process improvement, customer service, account management, or yes, even coaching and developing employees, all activities that should improve revenue. Even if we adjust the numbers downward to account for first-line supervisors who do not cost us $173 per hour, or assume that we can only save 25% of their time, or assume that the manager WILL spend the saved hours shopping on the Internet, the financial impact on managerial productivity is staggering! I believe that

Big Five Performance Management is a tool that is significant enough to help change the landscape of modern business productivity! And the best part for Human Resources professionals is that WE CAN LEAD THE WAY!

Human Resources people are always talking about making sure that HR has "a seat at the table," meaning that the HR Department and the HR professionals working in that department want to be considered as important, serious, valuable, collaborative colleagues and business partners by the business leaders in their company—the people who are actually making money for the company. So the question that arises is how do we, as HR professionals, expect to be taken seriously by our colleagues when we not only allow, but build on, codify, and perpetuate a very broken traditional annual performance assessment system? In my opinion, we are no better than the snake-oil salesmen of the old American West, peddling a remedy that we can hope to sell quickly, getting out of town before anyone becomes the wiser!

Big Five Performance Management provides an effective, common-sense, low-cost alternative to traditional annual performance assessment. Let this book serve as a call to action for Human Resources professionals and managers at all levels to improve this most fundamental process. Be a hero in your organization by introducing this process. When we accomplish this, we will not only have that "seat at the table," but we will actually deserve it. Finally, performance assessment that works!

Interested in pursuing *Big Five Performance Management* for your organization?

If you need assistance, have questions, or would like to share your experiences, feel free to contact us at www.isihrconsulting.com or www.bigfiveperformance.com. You can also follow the progress of companies installing this process on Facebook at "Big Five Performance Management."

• • •

APPENDIX A: EXAMPLES OF BIG FIVE PERFORMANCE MANAGEMENT MONTHLY REPORTS

Appendix A provides four examples of employee-prepared, monthly *Big Five Performance Management* reports prepared in e-mail format. The first two examples show *Big Five* in its most simple form, while the third demonstrates how easily organizations can add to and modify the basic format. The fourth example is included to illustrate how someone in an administrative position or other support role might still utilize *Big Five*.

Example One: Employee-Prepared *Big Five Performance Management* Report

This example is in its most simple form with only three categories: accomplishments, other accomplishments, and priorities for next month.

 John Smith
john.smith@acme.com

To
My Boss

Cc

John Smith *Big Five*: Feb/March 2014

February Accomplishments
1. Finalize and publish all the policy updates we discussed.
   Completed. All new policies published on February 22.
2. Meet with the vendor to get final estimates on training program.
   Final estimate routed to you on February 8. Suggest we negotiate a lower rate.
3. Resolve the Huntington Beach office bonus problem.
   Unresolved. Janet will not budge!
4. Continue to work with Julie to wrap up the Watson case.
   We met with the plaintiff's attorney, and they agreed to a settlement, thanks to Julie's persuasive arguments!
5. Find a challenging portfolio assignment for Steve.
   Steve will run the quarterly forum meetings for this year. I will work with him on the hand-off.

Other Accomplishments
- sales team closed the Fischer deal...outstanding work!
- finished the relocation proposal for Evan
- hosted Leon during his office visit
- conducted three orientation meetings with new employees

March Priorities

1. Share key learning from the Fischer deal in our staff meeting.
2. Continue to talk to Sheila about the reorganization. We will need a formal plan soon.
3. Corrective action for Kevin, now under quota for the third month in a row.
4. Call on our top five clients with the sales team to ask about the change in the software and how it might be affecting them.
5. Explore the possibility of partnering with Systems on the upcoming joint venture.

Example Two: Employee-Prepared *Big Five Performance Management* Report

This example shows how last month's priorities are copied and pasted into this month's accomplishments, creating month-to-month continuity.

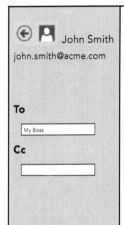

John Smith *Big Five:*
Mar/April 2014

March Accomplishments
1. Share key learning from the Fischer deal in our staff meeting.
   Prepared and presented 20-minute PowerPoint in our March 4 staff meeting. Bob had me present it again to the division team on March 15. It was a big home run!
2. Continue to talk to Sheila about the reorganization. We will need a formal plan soon.
   Our first meeting to formalize the plan is scheduled for April 12, as we discussed. The preliminary plan is on your desk for review.
3. Corrective action for Kevin, now under quota for the third month in a row.
   Completed. Formal corrective action has begun.
4. Call on our top five clients with the sales team to ask about the change in the software and how it might be affecting them.
   Called on only three of the five clients as the Fischer presentation took more time than I thought. So far, no complaints.

5. Explore the possibility of partnering with Systems on the upcoming joint venture. **Systems is not interested.**

Other Accomplishments
- attended the mandatory Safety class

April Priorities
1. Visit the remaining two clients regarding the software changes.
2. Follow-up on Kevin...ongoing.
3. Focus on any actions coming out of the reorganization plan as it will be the highest priority.
4. Call on our top five clients with the sales team to ask about the change in the software and how it might be affecting them.
5. Complete the process flow analysis and make a recommendation on changes by April 21.

Example Three: Employee-Prepared *Big Five Performance Management* Report

This example includes some sample metrics that might be important to the business unit and a sample "SOS" section, giving the employee an opportunity to ask for management's assistance.

John Smith John Smith
john.smith@acme.com

To
My Boss

Cc

John Smith *Big Five*: Mar/April 2014

Metrics
Volume: 382,423 units processed; 12 percent above budget
Quality; A–; per March report from Quality Assurance
Safety: Close Calls- 0; Incidents- 0; Lost Time- 0

March Accomplishments

1. Share key learning from the Fischer deal in our staff meeting.
   Prepared and presented 20-minute PowerPoint in our March 4 staff meeting. Bob had me present it again to the division team on March 15. It was a big home run!

2. Continue to talk to Sheila about the reorganization. We will need a formal plan soon.
   Our first meeting to formalize the plan is scheduled for April 12, as we discussed. The preliminary plan is on your desk for review.

3. Corrective action for Kevin, now under quota for the third month in a row.
   Completed. Formal corrective action has begun.

4. Call on our top five clients with the sales team to ask about the change in the software and how it might be affecting them.

Called on only three of the five clients as the Fischer presentation took more time than I thought. So far, no complaints.

5. Explore the possibility of partnering with Systems on the upcoming joint venture.
Systems is not interested.

Other Accomplishments
- attended the mandatory Safety class

April Priorities

1. Visit the remaining two clients regarding the software changes.
2. Follow-up on Kevin...ongoing.
3. Focus on any actions coming out of the reorganization plan as it will be the highest priority.
4. Call on our top five clients with the sales team to ask about the change in the software and how it might be affecting them.
5. Complete the process flow analysis and make a recommendation on changes by April 21.

SOS

May need your help with Huntington Beach. Janet is persistent!

Example Four: Employee-Prepared *Big Five Performance Management* Report

This is an example that might be prepared by someone in an administrative role who may not believe that they have anything worthy of reporting.

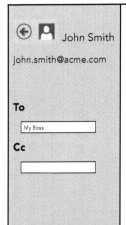 John Smith

john.smith@acme.com

To

My Boss

Cc

Annie Admin *Big Five*: Mar/April 2014

March Accomplishments

1. Adjusted my schedule to arrive early on Tuesdays and Thursdays to make certain that the materials for the staff meetings were compiled and distributed, per your request. Good idea!
2. Booked your Madrid trip for June and managed to get you on Marge Caldwell's schedule for dinner. I had to call in some favors on that one!
3. Settled a small dispute among the other admins about holiday scheduling. Let me know if you want to hear the details.
4. Followed up with the new vendor to make certain that the annual reports would be printed on time. Everything is on schedule.
5. Prepared three draft communications for your review and edits. I like that kind of work, so let me know if I can do more for you.

Other Accomplishments
- completed year-end filing project.
- worked with IT to automate the building's conference room scheduler. It should be turned on next month and help us avoid confusion over who is meeting where.

April Priorities

1. Do you think it would be a good idea to send Marge Caldwell a package for her to review prior to your dinner? Want me to put something together?
2. Continue to check on the printer to make sure there are no problems with the annual report.
3. Talk to Remy about possible training for the security people. We have had two complaints about rudeness this week.
4. Remember to ask your direct reports about their needs for summer interns, as several board members have called to ask.
5. Remember that I leave for Cancun on the 20th. Bill will be my replacement, and I will brief him thoroughly before I leave.

APPENDIX B: EXAMPLES OF MANAGER RESPONSES AND COACHING COMMENTS

This appendix provides samples of coaching comments that a manager might make in a typical *Big Five Performance Management* report response. They are presented to illustrate the wide range and diversity of possible responses, from simple encouragement and coaching to more formal corrective action. Note, please, that most contain at least one specific reference to something that the employee accomplished last month or plans to accomplish next month. Addressing concerns in this manner demonstrates that the manager has actually read the report and cares about the results!

Examples: Simple Manager Acknowledgment and Response

Effective managers will use *Big Five Performance Management* responses not only to acknowledge their employees' input but also to suggest process improvements or plant seeds for increased performance with their employees. For example, take a look at these relatively simple but effective comments:

"Great February, Ted! I especially liked the improvement in the volume numbers. Any success secrets you want to share with the other teams?"

"Go, Ted, go! Great report! Be sure to thank your team on my behalf!"

"You continue to impress, Ted! I especially appreciate the publication of the policy revisions! Have you thought about assigning someone to track that throughout the year so that it does not pile up at year-end? That might make for a good portfolio assignment for someone. Just thinking..."

"Please set up a meeting with the training vendor, as we need to nail this down. I would like to be personally involved. Also, I will send Julie a thank-you note and copy you! Nice work!"

"Good report. Let's talk this month about a succession plan for your unit. If you were to be promoted, would Steven be your first choice as your replacement?"

Examples: Manager Responses Providing Basic Coaching

But comments like those above will not help when an employee is underperforming. In those cases, the dialogue needs to take a more serious tone. In the examples below, direct instructions are provided and some communication around expectations is either stated or implied. The continual use of *Big Five Performance Management* will track and document compliance with the manager's request or instructions should the situation escalate, with the timeline of events built in as an integrated component. Corporate attorneys always want to see that timeline!

"Ted…I know you are proud of your accomplishments, but this monthly reporting exercise is supposed to be easy for you to prepare and easy for me to read. Please limit future reports to one page only. Ask Bob if you need assistance, as his are generally about what I am looking for in terms of content and length."

"Ted…the volume numbers you are reporting are not the same as the numbers reported by Accounting. Can you please get with Simone and determine the difference in the two reports. What happened? I need to know by Thursday, please, as I have a meeting with Bill that afternoon."

"I appreciate the fact that the Watson case will be settled out of court, but what controls have you put into place to make certain that this type of thing does not happen again? Please prepare a cause-and-effect document (two-page maximum, using the department template) showing what happened and what you are doing to prevent future issues. I need to share it with the division president. Thanks."

"Thanks for finally getting out those policy revisions. They have been on your monthly reports as priority items for several months now. Why did they take so long?"

"Having Steven run the quarterly forum meetings does not seem to be a "reward" for his past performance nor a challenge to see if he is ready for the next level. Isn't most of what is required simple scheduling and administration? See me, please, and let's discuss something more significant. I have a couple of ideas."

"I appreciate the information in your monthly report, Ted, but would remind you to add the Breckenridge account as a March priority, as we discussed. It is important that you stay focused on the revenue targets established for your group and not get distracted by the administrative portions of your job."

"Ted, good report! On an unrelated note, I know that completing expense reports is not the most interesting thing in your day, but Expense Control is complaining that you tend to hold too many reports until past the monthly deadline. They say that this distorts the monthly reporting process and could cause them to make adjustments to the budget that could hurt you at year-end. Please make sure that you submit future expense reports in a timely manner…within the thirty days required by policy. Thank you!"

Example: Manager Response Providing "Bad Attitude" Coaching

What do we do about employees with bad attitudes? You know the type. They always seem to meet their metrics, but they still manage to be a drain on the team and a burden to their management. What can a manager say in his or her *Big Five* response that will be meaningful to this type of employee? In cases like this, the manager should focus on the specific behaviors the manager has personally observed. No hearsay or secondhand information allowed.

High-quality feedback might look something like the following:

"Ted, I know we have discussed this, but I feel the need to document it in your *Big Five*. When you roll your eyes because someone makes a suggestion in the staff meeting, sigh loudly when you perceive that someone is running long in their presentation, fold your arms and argue with anyone who has a question about your team, and close your notebook loudly and abruptly at the end of the meetings, you send a definite negative message to me and to your colleagues. Please follow through on the actions we discussed to help repair your relationships with your colleagues. Thank you!"

Example: Manager Response Including an Overall Rating

If an organization feels it is necessary to assign an overall number, score, or value to an employee, managers can simply copy and paste something like the following into each of their monthly responses to employees. It might look like this:

___ 5- Greatly exceeded the accomplishments of monthly priorities

___ 4- Exceeded most monthly priorities

___ 3- Accomplished the agreed to monthly priorities as expected

✓ 2- Accomplished some of the monthly priorities but improvement is needed

___ 1- Unacceptable in the accomplishment of agreed upon priorities.

What is the most important improvement need for this employee in the upcoming month?

"While you have indicated that you completed all of his priorities for March, it is my opinion that the work was not completed according to the quality standards for the department. Specifically, the cause-and-effect document I asked you to prepare was nothing more than a paragraph saying that 'controls are in place and that this type of incident will not happen again.' While I appreciate the sentiment, the cause-and-effect document was not in a format that I could share with the division president, as I originally requested. Please follow instructions more completely in the future."

Example: Manager Response Including Formal Corrective Action
Finally, when employees are not responding to coaching, formal corrective action may be necessary. Once again, there is a delicate balance between serious coaching and corrective action, with the most significant difference being the intention of the manager. The manager coaches, generally speaking, to improve the performance of the employee. The manager escalates to corrective action when the goal is to have the employee either *move up* (significantly improve his or her performance) or *move out* (find another job). The degree to which the manager will want to do corrective action inside the *Big Five Performance Management* process will depend on the culture of the organization and the established processes for handling corrective action, of course, but it could look something like the following:

"Ted, as we discussed, you are expected to report to work at 8:00 a.m., per the established and published work hours for our team (HR Policy #100). My records indicate that you have been late for work seven times in the last two weeks. Your tardiness is having a negative effect on the team and hampering our ability to offer quality customer service to our clients. Please consider this as your first warning, per the company's three-step corrective action policy. Failure to report to work on time will result in a second warning or, depending on the circumstances, could be escalated up to and including termination. You are an important part of our team, Ted. Please take the necessary actions to comply with policy, and let me know if you are facing issues or circumstances that I might be able to assist you with. Thank you."

APPENDIX C: THE BENEFITS OF BIG FIVE PERFORMANCE MANAGEMENT

Chapter One discusses "The Dirty Dozen" challenges inherent in traditional, annual performance assessment. That list, however, is a summary of the most important issues only. If we dissect the process thoroughly, we find twenty-six major flaws. They are presented here with comments about how *Big Five* helps to managers and organizations eliminate these challenges. Use this information if you are attempting to convince your team that *Big Five* is a better alternative. See www.bigfiveperformance.com for additional, supplemental materials.

Challenge 1- Traditional, annual performance appraisal consumes too much managerial time.
The average manager spends 400 hours per year on this process, about 20% of their time.

Big Five Solution
Big Five can reduce that time commitment significantly, saving about 50% of that time or four hours per week. If employers

also adopt the *Big Five* philosophy regarding compensation, an additional two hours a week can be added to that total.

Challenge 2- The traditional process is too expensive... in managerial expense.

Calculating the expense of the managers' time is easy. Pick the average base pay rate of your management team; add benefits and bonus costs; divide that number by 2,080 (number of hours in a compensation work year); and you come up with the hourly cost for that manager. Multiply that annual cost by the 400 hours the managers spend on the process and you have a very impactful number. For example:

$85,000 Base annual rate for average manager at ACME

+21,250 Benefits cost at 25% of base pay

+ 3,000 Average annual bonus

= $109,250 Total annual manager's compensation

÷ 2,080 Number of annual work hours

$52.27 Hourly cost manager

x 400 Number of annual spent on appraisal

= $20,909 Managerial cost of the traditional, annual process

And this is for ONE manager only!

Big Five Solution

Using the numbers in the example above, Big Five will reduce the total managerial expense, saving somewhere between $10,454 (50%) and $15,682 (75%), per manager, per year. The macro implications of this number are incredible. After all, how many managers are employed at ACME? At your company?

In the US? Europe? The Far East? *Big Five* could alter global business productivity!

Challenge 3- The traditional process is too expensive... in lost opportunity.

The numbers quoted in Challenge Two do not account for how managers will use the extra time that *Big Five* will create for them.

Big Five Solution
If you assume that that time will now be devoted to sales, account management, customer service, research & development, employee development, process improvement, etc., the impact on managerial productivity is even more impressive!

Challenge 4- The traditional process is too expensive... in IT/systems.

What does a corporate Performance Assessment or Management system cost? The cost will depend on the features and complexity of the process but most top-of-the-line systems are six-figure expenditures.

Big Five Solution
Big Five can be administered through existing e-mail and word processing software. No additional systems are necessary. This makes *Big Five* ideal for small to mid-sized businesses that do not have established IT protocols for this purpose. For larger companies, the process can also be incorporated into larger Learning Management Systems (LMS), Performance Management Systems (PMS), or Human Resources Information Systems (HRIS).

Challenge 5- The Return-On-Investment (ROI) in the traditional process is very low.

If you consider the total expense of all the challenges above, you would think that companies would make certain that they are getting the best possible "bang for their buck." Not so. Basic Internet research shows that 85% of surveyed companies report that their performance management systems are only "moderately effective." You don't have to look far to confirm the research. Ask yourself or anyone at work what they think of the process? Most managers will tell you that there is very little value in the process and that they continue doing it, "because Human Resources requires it." Employees feel the same. It makes you wonder if anyone on the board of directors truly understands how much time their highly compensated managers are spending on this very outdated process.

Big Five Solution

There are a number of process reasons why *Big Five* is a better alternative, all appearing below. For now, consider the following simple fact. If *Big Five* was **only** as effective as traditional, annual performance assessment, it would still be a better option. It requires much less time and expense and, by definition, increases the ROI for the process. Factor in the belief that *Big Five* is even more effective than traditional, annual performance assessment and the ROI is even more significant.

Challenge 6- Corporate goals are difficult to translate into meaningful personal goals.

In most traditional systems, employees are asked to align their personal goals with those created at the corporate or department level.   This is sometimes difficult as the average engineer, administrative assistant, or accountant may not know how they can contribute to an oil company's corporate goal of "expanding our presence in the North Sea."

Big Five Solution
Big Five allows the employee and their manager to write goals that are many times more meaningful than those that are mandated by corporate.   Both parties should know the corporate goals, of course, and make any and all logical connections that they can when establishing priorities.   An absolute tie to corporate goals, however, is not always necessary.

Challenge 7- The business climate changes too quickly for annual goals to be meaningful.

Most of us have found that at the end of a performance assessment cycle that at least one or two of our goals are no longer meaningful.   Changes in technology, our own management team or structure, the competition, legislation, the business plan, the budget, and so on, happen so frequently that by the time we reach year end, some goals are no longer viable.

Big Five Solution
The monthly reporting structure of *Big Five* totally eliminates this problem.

Challenge 8- Mid-year review meetings don't happen.

In traditional appraisal, the answer to challenge 7 is the mid-year review, a short conversation between the employee and their manager, designed to check-in and make any necessary adjustments to the plan.   The problem with this plan is that mid-year reviews do not occur with any degree of regularity or consistency. The bottom line here is that unless HR monitors and reports the completion of the mid-year review, they just don't happen. In my experience, only about 20% of the meetings actually occur as planned and those are completed because the best managers make sure they do and the best employees push for the meeting. In other words, the 20% of the meetings that do occur are conducted between the managers and employees who probably need the process the least.

Big Five Solution
The monthly reporting structure of *Big Five* totally eliminates this problem.

Challenge 9- Annual feedback is a very dated concept.
Given the technology tools available to us today (Twitter, Facebook, LinkedIn, etc.), most employees are accustomed to instant feedback, not annual feedback. Generation Y employees will consider anything older than 30 days to be "yesterday's news."

Big Five Solution
No employee feedback will be older than about 30 days.

Challenge 10- Metrics are valuable but do not always tell the full story.
Most traditional appraisal systems attempt to establish metrics to measure the completion of goals and the success of the

employee. This makes sense for volume driven positions like those in sales or manufacturing, where metrics like volume/dollar output and scrap rates are significant factors. Most positions, however, do not lend themselves to this type of measurement. Metrics are valuable when they make sense but they do not always tell the full story. In my Human Resources career, I have had to terminate twice as many employees for policy violations, insubordination, and poor teamwork than those I terminated for not meeting their quotas or numerical targets.

Big Five Solution
Big Five certainly allows for numerical goals when they make sense but is flexible enough to be able to tell a more complete story about the employee's performance. Most annual performance assessment systems also allow this flexibility so it may be enough to say that *Big Five* does not make too much of a "philosophical fuss" over the connection between the employee's performance and the employee's metrics. *Big Five* works well in both environments; those where metrics are significant and those where they are not.

Challenge 11- Metrics can be manipulated by employees.
This challenge is best illustrated by the following theoretical telephone conversation.
"Hi Bob! I got your message about needing the extra 500 cases of paper. Do you mind if I wait until next Monday to turn that in? That will be the start of my new sales incentive period. And yes, it is my turn to buy lunch."

Big Five Solution
Like the solution to challenge 10 above, *Big Five* is flexible enough to include metrics when they are meaningful and provide other data when metrics are not as valuable.

Challenge 12- Metrics can also be manipulated by managers.
In some traditional appraisal systems, compensation is formula driven. A score of 4.6 on a performance appraisal will translate into a 4.6% pay increase or some other percentage based on a chart, scale, or template created by the company. Managers will almost always complete the reviews and then examine the pay increases for equity. To change the merit pay amounts requires a change in the appraisal score and some managers will adjust the actual appraisal in order to make the compensation fair and equitable. There is nothing ethically incorrect about that process as managers certainly need to be responsible for making fair and equitable pay decisions. The question becomes, why must managers do so much work to make the system effective?

Big Five Solution
Like the solution to challenges 10 and 11 above, *Big Five* is flexible enough to balance the numerical and non-numerical measures of employee performance.

Challenge 13- Traditional, annual performance appraisal is about compliance, not about coaching.
Don't believe it? Check with your own HR department. They will always track the process to see that appraisals have been

completed but they will rarely check the process for quality. The bottom line here is that HR wants to make sure the process has been completed. They do not have the time and manpower to monitor the quality of the process. As long as the process is completed, management and HR appear satisfied.

Big Five Solution
One of the coolest things about *Big Five* is that it actually CREATES coaching! All of us have worried, at one time or another, about when we were going to be able to carve out time to develop our employees. The monthly reporting structure of *Big Five* creates ten documented coaching opportunities per month, per employee. Forget about your separate coaching initiative! Just incorporate *Big Five* into your monthly reporting for immediate results.

Challenge 14- The December struggle to remember what happened last January.
In annual appraisal systems, employees and managers both spend time and effort trying to reconstruct the events that occurred twelve months ago. "Did that happen this year or last year?"

Big Five Solution
The monthly reporting structure of *Big Five* totally eliminates this problem. Most *Big Five* users record their accomplishments daily on a white board, iPad, or some other visual method that keeps their priorities front-and-center during the

month. This makes final report preparation easy, taking as little as five minutes per month per employee.

Challenge 15- The proximity of most recent events.

The December struggle in challenge 14 means that many times managers will evaluate employees on what they have accomplished most recently, disregarding what may have happened, positive or negative, at the first of the year.

Big Five Solution
The monthly reporting structure of *Big Five* totally eliminates this problem.

Challenge 16- The "lean at the tape."

Like track stars straining to break the tape at the end of a race, some employees will step up their performance when appraisal time draws near.

Big Five Solution
The monthly reporting structure of *Big Five* totally eliminates this problem.

Challenge 17- Most managers are not good at employee confrontation.

Let's face it. Most of us do not enjoy having to provide constructive feedback in annual performance appraisals. No one likes being the bad guy. Even the managers who are very good at it expend a lot of time documenting, prepping, and worrying about the outcome.

Big Five Solution

Big Five cannot totally eliminate this challenge but it can help. The fact that the employee creates the priorities in *Big Five* means that the manager's job should be easier, simply determining if the employee accomplished the priorities or not. But that will not help us with the proverbial "problem child" that all of us seem to encounter at one time or another. In those cases, the *Big Five* structure continues to assist as feedback is given in monthly, bite-sized chunks versus the extreme of having the employee feel "dumped on" at year end. The ongoing monthly dialogue created by *Big Five* helps to ease the pain in most situations.

Challenge 18- Employees are not good at receiving constructive criticism.

Regardless of the manager's good intentions, most employees don't enjoy hearing bad news. Even if the relationship between the employee and the manager is a very good one, it is many times difficult for employees not to take the message as a personal affront to their character and good name. This is especially true if the negative feedback may be tied to a negative compensation decision. It is just human nature.

Big Five Solution

Like the response in challenge 17, the monthly reporting structure of *Big Five* will build a continual dialogue of coaching so that constructive feedback becomes the norm, a part of each monthly report. That feedback begins to feel more like guidance than correction.

Challenge 19- No employee enjoys knowing that they are "average" performers... or worse.

In many traditional appraisal systems an overall score, grade, or rating is determined for each employee. This is especially present in systems that formulate pay increase percentages based on appraisal scores. The very first thing the employee does after leaving the appraisal meeting is to check with co-workers to see how they compare. No one enjoys the discovery that they are an average or below average performer. That knowledge rarely spurs the underperforming employee to greater heights. In many cases, employees in this category begin to slow the pace of their work, cause problems with other team members, or begin looking for another job. And what is worse than an employee who quits and leaves? The employees who quits and stays!

Big Five Solution

Big Five evaluates employees in terms of what they have accomplished and makes no attempt to assign an overall grade, value, or score to the employee.

Challenge 20- Employee performance is not the most significant driver in determining merit pay increases.

The most significant driver is the amount of money the company has approved for increases. Managers spend a considerable amount of time allocating their annual merit increase budgets between employees in order to reward higher level performers and maintain equitable pay. This would, on the surface, appear to be a noble and worthwhile use of time. In most cases it is not. Assuming the company has approved a merit increase budget of 4%, for example, the managers will spend an incredible amount of time determining which employees receive 4.2% and which will receive only 3.8%, for example. The difference to the employee, after taxes, can be negligible and the exercise consumes far more time than it is worth.

Big Five Solution
It is recommended that employers adopt a merit increase system that provides any employee not on some sort of probation with a standard, across-the-board increase, much like a Cost Of Living Adjustment (COLA). Do not advertise the increase as a COLA, just call it this year's merit increase. Reserve a portion of the approved budget, let's say 1% in our example, for discretionary bonuses for the top 20% of employees. So in this example, the board of directors approves a 4% increase. The company announces that this year's merit increase will be 3% and reserves the 1% for bonuses for high level performers. This solution will save a tremendous amount of managerial time and will, most likely, produce results that are very similar to your current process. Admittedly, this recommendation attempts to make simple and quick work of a somewhat complex process. Still, the basic calculation of ROI for this process must be considered. See Chapter 6 for a more thorough discussion. Finally, *Big Five* will serve as a viable replacement for your current performance assessment system, even if you elect not to change the way you administer merit increases.

Challenge 21- Traditional annual performance appraisal is not an employee driven process.

Even in systems where the employee completes their own review to begin the process and would appear to take an active role in its ownership, this is still a company driven processes that means very little to most employees.

Big Five Solution
Big Five forms a monthly dialogue and partnership between the employee and the manager. It is a much more collaborative process than traditional, annual performance appraisal.

Challenge 22- At some point in the management hierarchy, the process breaks down.

In most organizations practicing traditional, annual performance assessment, the process stops at some level in the organization. Do you think that the Chairman of the Board prepares an appraisal for the CEO of your company? Doubtful. In most organizations the CEO does not even prepare them for his/her direct reports. After all, the typical CEO would argue that they have almost daily conversations with their direct reports, continually guiding and directing the outcomes. This may or may not be the case but the point is that a department manager is going to find it difficult to take the process seriously if that department manager completes appraisals on their direct reports but is not formally appraised by their boss. At some point, the process breaks down and the integrity of the program suffers.

Big Five Solution
Big Five will probably not prevent this type of breakdown. The difference is that the breakdown won't tend to harm the integrity of the program because employees at almost all levels will continue to see and believe in the value that *Big Five* brings. In other words, most employees will no longer care about who is not completing their *Big Five* because they find value in completing it themselves. The process is no longer about compliance but about accomplishment. And this sense of accomplishments feeds the fire as employees begin to compete with themselves, and others, to produce better and better results each month.

Challenge 23- Employees are skeptical of the traditional, annual appraisal process.
Research shows that 45% of employees surveyed said that their annual appraisals did not provide them with honest feedback about their job performance. Over 50% said that the process did not actually help them improve their performance. Once again, what is the ROI on this process? The traditional process can actually damage employee morale.

Big Five Solutions
As difficult as it might be to imagine, employees actually like *Big Five*! It helps them to better manage their time. It helps improve communication between the employee and their boss. It enables employees to take credit for their accomplishments in the workplace. It takes less time than the annual process. It works!

Challenge 24- Traditional, annual performance assessment can create corporate liability.

Because of the difficulties inherent in the traditional appraisal process, the ones detailed above, managers are sometimes less than truthful in providing feedback to employees. When this occurs, "soft" appraisals result as the existing manager decides that dealing with Barbara is just too difficult and not worth the time. A new manager finally takes over and decides that Barbara is a substandard employee and wants to terminate her. The termination occurs, Barbara engages the Equal Employment Opportunity Commission due to her race/age/gender, and we are off to court. What documentation does Barbara have to support her "unlawful termination" claim? It is not unusual for her attorney to present five years of traditional performance appraisals, all showing at least acceptable and sometimes even good performance. It is easy to see why a jury might think that the new manager "had it in" for Barbara.

Big Five Solution
Feedback in *Big Five* is very specific and focused on the accomplishment of priorities. Managers can certainly deviate from that path by writing extraneous comments but the primary focus of the process should help limit feedback to priorities and accomplishments; much more defendable in litigation.

Challenge 25- Rater bias.

In systems that formulate pay based on appraisal score, rater bias is an obvious problem. Some managers are tougher, or more truthful, than others. How do we insure fairness and equity across raters?

Big Five Solution
Big Five makes no attempt to assign an overall rating or score to an employee and does not attempt to formulate pay increases based on appraisal scores. Bias is not an issue.

Challenge 26- The single purpose nature of the traditional, annual performance appraisal.

What happens after annual appraisals are completed and merit increases are communicated? The documentation produced during this process continues to reside in the company's HR systems and/or the appraisal document is filed in the employee's personnel file. The issues raised in one appraisal should logically carry over but this year's improvement needs don't always make their way into concrete goals for the next year. Does the document serve any other purpose? Do managers who are hiring internally go to the personnel file to look at the employee's past reviews when they are considering an internal candidate from another department? In over 30 years of work as an HR professional I have only been asked to produce prior copies of an internal candidate's last performance appraisals three times! When I asked other managers if I needed to do that for them they told me it was not necessary. They already knew the candidate's current manager and doubted that past appraisals would tell them much. Talk about an indictment on the process!

Big Five Solution
The cyclical nature of *Big Five*, reporting each month on progress made against ongoing priorities, provides a logical flow of information from month to month, ensuring that no priority is forgotten.

Are there other issues you would like to add? See our Facebook page at *Big Five Performance Management* to contribute.